Also by David Altshuler

Raising Healthy Kids in an Unhealthy World

Love the Kid You Get. Get the Kids You Love

Kids Learn What They Live.

Kids Live What They Learn.

All inquiries should be addressed to:
David Altshuler
4520 SW 62 Avenue
Miami, FL 33155
305 663-9394

www.DavidAltshuler.com
David@Altshulerfamily.com

ISBN-13: 978-1530364367
ISBN-10: 1530364361

To my beloved family

Acclaim for

Kids Learn What They Live:
Kids Live What They Learn

I am thrilled that David is publishing a third volume of his wisdom and wit. He has a way of making you want to read things that you may not want to hear but know in your heart to be true. In a day when common sense seems to be in short supply, David provides clinical and, more importantly, practical truth in an easy to swallow dose of delightfully worded essays. I look forward to reading everything David writes and am honored to consider him my friend.

David H. Craig, Ph.D., Psychologist,
Executive Director of The King's Daughters' School, TN

When David finishes writing a book, I am ready to ask him when the next one is coming! That anticipation demonstrates how much I respect David's knowledge and understanding of children and their families, and how I appreciate his special gift of putting that understanding to paper in a way that shares his great compassion and caring for these families. His analogies are uplifting and humorous, and yet, we can see ourselves and our shortcomings as parents in page after page of his stories.

Because I run a residential treatment center for young adults, I love to provide David's books as a resource to our families. Even though our clients are young adults, they often cling to their folks as though they were still much younger kids, (often with a maturity level of a 20 year old going on 14), thus wanting all the privileges of adulthood but not at all ready to handle life as an adult. Families more often than not, know that they are contributing to the dysfunctional process of the dance that is going on between parent and child, yet they struggle with being able to change this dynamic.

They want help. David's books help our families, who still need the support, insight, and road maps to help them gain the tools that they need at this time in their parenting life. I remind them that these books are to be used as daily tools, to be brought out again and again to help them when they are struggling with the concepts of when to hold on and when to let go.

Jayne Longnecker-Harper, M.Ed.,
Founder and CEO of Benchmark Transitions, CA

If you are a parent, or if you are thinking of ever becoming a parent, now is the time to start reading David Altshuler's compassionate insights, which he shares with just the right balance of wit and outrage. David's latest book builds on the themes of his blog posts and secures his place as a natural-born storyteller. Based on decades of real-world experience as a classroom teacher, educational consultant and college counselor (not to mention his role as the father of four), David challenges parents to embrace and guide their children with unfettered concern for their well-being. That means being physically and mentally present (try getting down and dirty with your kids in the outdoors), setting limits (just say no to 24/7 access to electronics) and otherwise creating an environment in which young people can grow and thrive and find some downtime in a fast-paced world filled with skewed values.

Patty Shillington, Parent

David and his most recent work are a true unity of love and passion for the kids with whom he works. He brings "fierce compassion" to his work. He is open, honest, and forthcoming with families. He addresses complex issues providing the best possible placement outcomes. David goes through the trials and tribulations of adolescent behaviors gently and attentively as he gracefully crosses another marathon line with his whimsical sense of humor and gracious advice.

Andrey Rossin, CEO and Founder, IntoAction Treatment, FL.

Anyone who reads David's work will quickly grasp his deep understanding of family. Practical, philosophical, compassionate and humorous, I always enjoy David's work.

Patrick M. Finn, Director of Enrollment, Foxcroft School, VA

Kids Learn What They Live makes parents and professionals frequently think, "That is soo true!! I've made a similar mistake myself. I am so glad to know I've now been awakened to the most powerful way to be a more effective parent." After reading this book, you will be inspired to LIVE in a way that will help your children LIVE their lives the right way."

Mike Domitrz, Producer & Host of "HELP! My Teen Is Dating.
Real Solutions to Tough Conversations" DVD and Founder of
www.DateSafeProject.org

Parenting might remain more art than science. Go with your gut; believe in yourself; learn from your mistakes. No one is taught how to parent, we all learned at our parents' feet – promising "I'll never make my child do (fill in the blank)!" and less often we have the pleasure (those of us who are past parenting and enjoying the next generation) of seeing our kids do just what we did, with thanks. But along the way we have all needed a little (sometimes a lot of) guidance – from the pediatrician, from our friends, our parents, or books. The "lessons" arrive in the form of stories, really contemplations and observations delivered in plain, non-judgmental language, with a large dose of common sense and good will. David has a warm, heartfelt style, that comes from his own experience – in his family, and as the consultant to hundreds of other families who have sought his counsel. Join them and benefit from the time spent with David.

Jerome Poliacoff, Ph.D., Child and Family Psychologist,
Working Exclusively With High Conflict Families and
Difficult Children in South Florida

David's third book *Kids Learn What They Live* is a must read for parents or anyone involved with kids. I love David's wit and humor in addressing factors that are affecting the core of our society--the family. I have known David for over 15 years and have worked collaboratively with him in placing adolescents and young adults in programs I have worked for. David's approach of compassion and gentle guidance have helped many parents make the difficult decision of placing their children in treatment. His advice, based on knowledge, wisdom and experience, have helped many families. I am grateful he is willing to share this expertise.

Gay Jackson, RN, Outreach and Admissions,
New Roads Behavioral Health, Cottonwood Heights, Utah

"Insightful commentary on child-raising that every parent can use! Dave's 30-plus years of watching and working with parents comes through in a down-to-earth way that relies on real-life experience minus all the psychobabble. This is a book that even the parent who doesn't see the need for advice can connect with and gain value from. This work is a one-of-a-kind in a crowded market of similar books, but stands out for is easy-read, entertaining style."

Brent R. Hall, LMFT, Executive Director
Discovery Academy, Discovery Connections

In his newest book, Kids Learn What They Live, David continues to write in his confident and caring voice as a beacon of hope, offering guidance in an ever increasingly busy and noisy world. Although I prefer to read short sections of his books at a time, in order to digest the provocative ideas he stirs up, it is hard to not read this book cover to cover. I find myself hungry to keep reading, both professionally as an educator of 26 years, and personally as a parent of almost two decades. The messages David conveys are in direct alignment with how I try to lead my school and parent my own children. His humor, anecdotes, and honest reflections create a disarming tone throughout his text, making it easy to hear what

David has to say. Slow down, relax, take a breath. Appreciate our kids for who they are, appreciate ourselves for who we are. I am ok, you are ok, we are ok – we are on this journey together. Thank you, David, for sharing your wisdom.

C.J. Spirito, Head of School, Rock Point School, Burlington, VT

What I always appreciate about David's approach to parenting and educational consulting is his no nonsense approach. In todays" trophy-syndrome" society where no one ever loses and everyone wins a prize, David is able to cut through the babble and offer thought-provoking ideas and solutions. He does so with a witty sense of humor, which makes his written work an absolute joy to read. I wish every parent would read this book.

Marek Pramuka, Director of Admissions and Marketing, The Storm King School, Cornwall on Hudson, New York

Kids Learn What They Live.

Kids Live What They Learn

David Altshuler, M.S.

Langley Press

Table of Contents

Kids Learn What They Live.

Kids Live What They Learn.

David Altshuler, M.S.

Langley Press

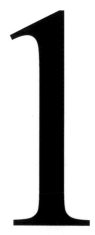

You Can't Spell Love Without "Involved"

Parents trying to raise healthy kids in our toxic culture frequently describe how alone they feel: "All the other parents let their kids play vacuous, violent, addictive video games." Parents also feel overwhelmed. "We both have jobs. Do you know what it costs to live in this city?" Parents feel stunned into submission. "We can't take off work to be at home policing our child's every interaction with the computer." Parents also feel conflicted: "The kid needs the computer to do Internet research and send in homework. How are we supposed to know if he spends a few minutes playing violent, addictive, video games?"

In actuality, parents make choices like the one about whether or not to allow video games all the time. Indeed, it could be argued that as parents, making decisions about what are kids are going to do is one of our primary responsibilities.

From potty training (we don't pee in the living room) to choice of high school (our morning commute does not involve the suburbs of Paris) parents help kids to make the choices that reflect the values of the family. You are able--required--to make suggestions about where your kids pee. Why do you feel helpless to help them determine whether or not they will be at risk for living in your basement until they're 30 years old because all they know how to do is play vacuous, violent, addictive, video games and did I mention that last time I checked the want ads nobody was looking to hire somebody with strong thumbs, no skills, and a predilection for slaughtering graphic ogres in a glowing rectangle?

The other half of the equation is that there needs to be an attractive alternative to vacuous, violent, addictive, video games. I wouldn't want to make the case, "You can't play violent, addictive video games" and then go on to say, "And you can't do anything else fun either, now go sit in your room by yourself and solve an algebra problem or something." Love includes involvement. Love means never having to say, "You've played 'League of Legends' for three hours today already, I told you to do your homework, I need a drink" because you already took your kid hiking or drove her and her friend to the bank of the river and watched them cavort and push each other into the water. You can go ahead and return an email while you watch them play for all I care.

2

If you can't be home to cook dinner, at least you can make sure that your kids eat McBlech only occasionally. If you can't be involved in tossing a ball or going on a hike or bringing a cooler to the beach or playing a board game or renting a cabin in the woods, then AT LEAST ensure that the kids aren't playing violent, addictive video games.

Or as the Keanu Reeves character said in "Parenthood:" "... you need a license to buy a dog or drive a car. Hell, you need a license to catch a fish. But they'll let any [expletive deleted] be your father."

Surely, we can do better than that.

No matter how alone, overwhelmed, and stunned we may feel.

Can't We Agree To Agree?

Over breakfast recently, I mentioned in an overtly casually-pass the toast-sort of tone that I needed to travel to Northern Virginia to tour boarding schools.

"Where's the marathon?" my long-suffering wife responded without looking up.

"I'm sure I don't know what you're talking about," I replied. "Ethical independent consultants have to consistently update their knowledge of traditional boarding schools around the country. A colleague of mine who was the director of admissions at one of my favorite New Hampshire schools recently became the head of a school in Virginia and I feel a responsibility to my clients to..."

"Where's the marathon?" Patti repeated in the same steady voice that has caused many a fifth grader on the playground over the years to P-U-T T-H-A-T R-O-C-K D-O-W-N R-I-G-H-T N-O-W.

"What in the world makes you think that there's a marathon this time of year in Northern Virginia? Sometimes, I honestly just can't figure out how you get ideas in your head."

Patti was silent, but gave me "the look."

Clearly beaten, I fessed up: "It's the marathon of the Potomac," I admitted. That the packet pickup for the race is actually in D.C. rather than in Northern Virginia scored me no husband points whatsoever; I decided that "right now" would be an exceptionally propitious time to clear out those palm fronds and attend to a number of other tasks calling to me from the back yard.

In short, Patti saw straight through me. Were my forehead made of glass, she could not have been more accurate about my intention. I frequently plan my touring of colleges and boarding schools to correspond with local running events and she knows it. Some people like to play golf courses around the country; I like to see what the locals are doing at 26.2. Surely, traveling to the 48 contiguous states to check out indigenous meth labs would be worse.

But the point is that family members--your kids in particular--don't have to channel the Amazing Kreskin to know your opinion of matters ranging from studying to housework to promiscuity to underage drinking. They know what you think. The $64,000 question involves how to help our kids come to agree that our point of view involving sober attention to academics should take precedence over the prevailing opinion in our culture--that "fat, drunk, and stupid is [the] way to go through life."

Imagine, if you would, just how violently unpleasant it would be if you were forced to listen to political, social, or religious views in direct contrast to those which you hold dear. Perhaps you don't have to think back any further than a recent trip to an airport waiting room or your dentist's office. Pretty miserable, huh? Those talking heads pontificating endlessly about how the president is right (or wrong), the course we should follow in the middle east (or not), and how our immigration policy in the American Southwest is correct (or isn't.) Maddening, no?

You already know what those crackpots think. Their views are ubiquitous. The REASON you don't invite opinionated Republicans (or Democrats), Sunnis (or Shias), non-runners (or runners) to breakfast is that they are they don't agree with you. People with disparate points of view are welcome to engage in informed discussion at the evening meal, but please, not at breakfast.

If your kids are living in a home where they are constantly subjected to a barrage of views that contradict their own experience, they are likely to shut out their parents. And who could blame them? Thumper's advice applies to your children as much as to animated animals. "If you can't say something nice, don't think your kids want to hear it repeatedly."

Or more succinctly: What makes you think that telling your son to do his homework for the one hundred and first time is going to make all the difference?

Kill the Ref

Can you imagine? A gentle reader suggested to this author recently that I am harsh and--gasp!--judgmental. My thoughtful critic went on to say that I give advice (if I remember correctly, the word "pontificate" was bandied about like undergarments on a clothesline) but offer no viable solutions and that what I recommend is as cliché as it is unlikely. "To model sobriety for our kids, you want us parents not to drink?" my friend sputtered. "And you're always telling us to have fun with our kids--to read to them rather than let them play 'Shoot, Shoot, Shoot, Blood, Blood, Blood, Kill, Kill, Kill.' Are you kidding? When do I have time to help them make a lemonade stand? Did it ever occur to you that I have a job?"

With these thoughtful criticisms in mind, I am going to target low-hanging fruit in this essay. I am going to selflessly eviscerate parents who scream at the referees at their daughter's soccer games. I hope my temperate readers will agree with my characterization of these boors. (I'll go back to marginally harder targets--parents who smoke pot with their kids--in subsequent essays.)

You know the one I mean: there's the guy pacing the sidelines invoking ancient and modern deities to smite the referee. "Kill the ref" he begins in the first period of play then escalates to harsher suggestions as the game--swarms of adorable lemmings massing around a slow moving soccer ball--continues.

Charitably, the man only wants what is best for his daughter. Arguably he believes that his daughter cares about winning as much as he does. Unfortunately, he is wrong on both counts.

"Everybody gets the same cards" is as true in poker as it is for seven-year-olds playing soccer. Unless you are a member of the 1927 New York Yankees, the odds are that in the long run you--and your offspring--will have just as many Ws as Ls. As the law of large numbers is unlikely to be repealed any time soon, isn't it important to teach our children how to win and lose gracefully and with character?

Rather than screaming at the ref--typically a high school kid earning $20 per game--a better message for dad to communicate might be: "Play hard, play fair, go home."

8

Because it's important to distinguish between how the rabid parent and the young player perceive what is transpiring on the field. In grown up world, winning isn't everything, it's the only thing. Or as Vince Lombardi said, "if winning isn't important, why do they keep score?"

In kid world on the other hand, your daughter may be more interested in developing skills. And even the most rabid Packers fan would admit that there were no seven-year-olds on that 1967 team that won all those games. Your daughter may be learning social cues from the other young people. She is certainly interested in your perceptions and reactions. She is eager for your approval and affection.

Win or lose.

Ultimately, the question is whether or not you want to impose your worldview on your young child. Inflicting your values is best done with someone who respects and admires you. It's hard for your little one to admire a person who is psychotically yelling at a 17-year-old in a striped yellow shirt. She would be more likely to value your guidance and advice if there was less spittle frothing from your gaping mouth.
"Love your kids for who they are not for what they do" can hardly be exemplified better than by your calm acceptance of the path your child is walking on the soccer pitch.

And what if your daughter has no interest whatsoever in competitive athletic games? Would you have the good sense to allow her to stay home with you cuddled up on the couch reading books? I certainly hope so. It is my fervent wish that you would allow your daughter to be who she is.

Bad Trip

Last night I dreamt I was trapped at a dinner party where a woman whom I did not know, apropos of nothing, addressed me as follows:

"It is beyond my understanding why the fascist authorities insist on restricting my civil rights and try to forbid me from driving 70 miles per hour. I so don't get it. How is how fast I drive anyone's business but my own? I understand that 70 miles per hour is 40 miles per

10

hour over the speed limit. But here's my point: driving 70 miles per hour isn't nearly as dangerous as driving 90 miles per hour. Ninety miles per hour is 60 miles per hour over the speed limit. Ninety miles per hour is much worse than 70. All the studies say so. The research is unequivocal. There is nothing to argue about: driving 90 miles per hour is more dangerous than driving 70 miles per hour.

"Why is everyone making such a big deal out of my driving 70 miles per hour? I don't deny that there are two school zones on my route to work in the morning. But driving 90 miles per hour would be much more dangerous for those elementary school age kids than the 70 miles per hour that I drive.

"The police, the legislators, and the parents in the neighborhood are all so stupid. They want to turn the clock backward. What do these reactionaries want? Do they want everyone to drive ten miles per hour? Two hundred years ago, ten miles an hour was the fastest that anyone could travel because that's how fast a horse could go. But I don't have a horse; I have a 400-horse power engine. Don't these people understand that we can't go backward as a culture? Isn't it clear that I should be allowed to drive 70 miles per hour because I can?

"If I weren't supposed to drive 70 miles per hour, then why do I have a car that can go 70 miles per hour? Don't the authorities understand this obvious point? And as I keep pointing out, driving 90 miles an hour would be worse.

"We are a nation of laws, not a nation of obligations. Our country is about what I can do-not about what I have to do or ought to do. If these children in the school zone want to stay safe then they need to play somewhere else or go to school somewhere else. I like driving 70 miles per hour. Yes sometimes, I get a speeding ticket, but I always pay it. So what's the problem?"

I woke up screaming.

At the risk of "explaining the joke," ("explaining the dream"?) here's a similar argument to the one above: Marijuana should be legalized because marijuana is not as dangerous as alcohol or cigarettes.

I find this "not as dangerous as" argument equal parts infuriating and vacuous in that falling off a 300-foot cliff is, in some sense I suppose, "better" than falling off a 400-foot cliff.

But not a great deal better in that dead is dead.

This "not as dangerous as" argument is the best argument for the pro-marijuana forces? Really? That's the best they've got? That marijuana is less dangerous than alcohol-which is responsible for countless needless deaths every year-and less dangerous than cigarettes-which are responsible for even more needless deaths?

The speaker above argues that children in the school zones should get out of her way to avoid being run over when she is driving 40 miles per hour over the speed limit. Similarly, proponents of legalization suggest that their right to smoke pot trumps a child's right to grow up without infinite access to pot. I call this the "I'll only pee on my side of the pool" argument. Legalized marijuana means easier access to pot for everyone, including children.

Everybody knows about your cousin, the successful neurosurgeon in the Midwest who smokes pot on the weekend yet functions beautifully in the operating room during the week. But just because someone survives a fall from a great height is a poor argument in favor of jumping off a cliff to enjoy the view on the way down. Many kids who smoke pot become addicted and have concomitant problems including school failure, oppositionality, and depression-problems that they wouldn't have had absent their dependence on marijuana. Just because you can smoke pot with impunity doesn't mean that they can. Just because somebody wins the lottery every week doesn't mean that you should sell your house to invest in lotto tickets.

What are loving parents to do? The choice is clear: keep your kids away from addictive drugs. Replace the temptations with other choices-almost any other choices will do. My dad and I used to toss a baseball when I was growing up; my mom and I used to go to the library. But I commend to your attention gardening, baking, athletics, woodworking, hiking, board games, swimming, fishing, canoeing, camping, travel, and volunteer work.

Among others.

Also, keep the stress level down. Don't push your kids relentlessly down the academic road to nowhere. Wouldn't you rather have a happy, well-adjusted, drug free child than a stressed out, stoned, recalcitrant one with better grades? Wouldn't you rather have a neighbor who observes the speed limit in the school zone rather than selfishly insisting that at least driving 70 miles per hour is better than careening along at 90 mph?

5

Helpful Running

As dedicated readers of my books are endlessly aware, I have been running with the same group of balding, paunchy, sweaty, middle-aged folks for a number of decades now. Older, slower, stiffer though we may be, our group has survived the disruption of hurricanes, the ravages of divorce, and half a dozen presidential campaigns. What has kept us together after all these years? (I'm going to eliminate "pure and utter madness" from among the answer choices.)

Clearly, we all share a predilection for this (allegedly) healthy pursuit. And, obviously, one of the "costs of entry" is the willingness to get up early and put in some miles. But there is no consensus about any other demographic: Our members do not share political affiliation, gender, race, social class or any other criteria. We are democrats or republicans; we are wealthy or middle class; we are religious observers or atheists; we have children or not.

One of us recently suggested that what brought us together and what keeps us together is a shared willingness to listen to endless repetition of the same bad jokes ("Did you hear the one about the interrupting cow?") Again, I am going to discount this possibility as too horrible to think about.

My insight into what keeps us together running through this murky swamp in the dark is our mutual conviction that the good of the group takes precedence over the well-being of any individual member. Our concern for one another trumps our concern for ourselves. My buddy, Tim, for example has completed over 30 marathons and has qualified for the Boston Marathon many times over the course of 40 years of running. He is as fit as any 66 year-old on the planet. Yet he has never once begun a sentence with a first person pronoun. Every conversation with Tim begins with his inquiring, "How is your training coming along?" "When is your next event?" "Can I be of help to you in achieving your running goals?"

Lorna just returned from South Africa where she participated in a 56-mile event. (No, that is not a typo. At 56 miles, Comrades is among the toughest distance events ever.) Although she has a great deal of which to be proud-including having run marathons on all seven continents-she never brags. Like Tim, Lorna begins every conversation with "How is your running going?" "How can I be of help?"

Kelly, a cancer survivor, saw a shirt logo, "If you think training for a marathon is hard, try chemo." She thought for a moment and said, "No, when I was in the hospital, people brought me food and took care of me. Running the marathon was harder." Her good spirits and accomplishments inspire us all.

Those of us who run marathons in four and a half hours admire those who run marathons in three and a half hours: "How do you run so fast?" Those of us who run marathons in three and a half hours admire those of us who run marathons in five and a half hours. "How can you stay out on the course for so long?"

In a torrential rainstorm in the days before cell phones, a half dozen of us showed up at the appointed place-in the downpour, in the dark. "I might not care about myself enough to get out of bed and work out in this deluge, but I'm not going to disappoint my buddies" was the unspoken consensus.

What do all these miles, meetings and conversations have to do with keeping our children safe in a world increasingly hostile to developing minds and bodies? A lifelong love of words begins with hearing cooing and giggling sounds at birth; a lifelong love of reading begins with being read to from an early age; and a lifelong love of healthful exercise begins with play, play, and more play from the time your beloved child first learns to walk.

If your young daughter is miserable at soccer (is the coach more concerned about winning than about developing skills? Are the other parents yelling "kill the ref"?) it might be time for some unstructured play. If organized sports are more organized and less sport, let's consider moving on to hiking, biking, running, or canoeing. Whatever you do, get those kids off the couch. (Did you throw away your TV like I told you to in my last book?)

As with so many activities, peers are critical. It's hard to be the kid who likes tromping around in the outdoors if all the other kids want to hang out at the mall and slurp sucrose. I promise that there are still some children who want to join yours in looking up at the sky after an evening hike. My fondest wish for you and your kids is that you are able to help them find a group with the Tims, Lornas, and Kellys of your neighborhood.

Enough is Enough

This chapter will be just as helpful without the joke—equal parts old, offensive, and terrible—in the following paragraph:

Having fasted for three days waiting in the snow, the woman is told by the disciples that she may finally speak to the great guru whom she has traveled half a world to see. "But he is busy," the devotees go on. "Each penitent may speak only four words to his eminence." Bowing, the woman approaches the throne and says, "Sheldon. Enough is enough."

How much is enough in your house? Do your children have unfettered access to media of all kinds? Because the only way they can get an iPad, television, computer, PlayStation or other device is through you. Reasonable people can disagree about whether or not a child should have her inheritance at 25 or 35 years of age. But no rational person would argue that a ten-year-old should be empowered to make decisions about the disposal of his fortune. ("We had hoped Percy would continue to invest in the index fund that his great-grandfather founded, but instead he bought ten million dollars' worth of Pringles potato chips. No, not Pringles' stock. The actual potato chips. He has rented a storage unit. A few storage units actually. Ten million dollars buys a lot of potato chips.") Kids that young don't have money. If they're playing video games, it's because you, their parents, have allowed and encouraged. You are a Quisling. You are responsible.

I'm not judging you; I'm not throwing a stone at you; I'm not saying that you have abdicated one of your most fundamental responsibilities as a loving parent. I'm just suggesting that the research is clear: you know those treatment centers for video game addiction? Kids who don't play video games don't get to go to them. Screens of all kinds can be problematic for some kids. You don't want to gamble that your kid is one for whom screens will have a significant negative influence. Parents have to step up and help their children make some easy decisions. You don't allow your pre-adolescent child to watch XXX-rated pornography. (Or if you do, don't bother reading the rest of this chapter. We are on opposite sides of such a high fence that there is nothing for us to discuss.) Why would you let them choose what shows to watch? Especially when there is so much good stuff already out there.

If you insist of allowing your children to watch television—and I am the first to admit that it's hard not to—can you at least set the standard for what is appropriate? There are enough television shows. More than enough. For every one hour of you tube video that your child watches, there are 6000 more hours of content created. You don't let your child have ice cream for breakfast, lunch and dinner every single day, why would you allow her to choose to watch inappropriate images infinitely?

Especially when there are—stop me if I've used this word before— enough shows that are NOT filled with violent, disjointed images that give me a headache just thinking about them. I'm not sure that I can sell you, gentle reader, on the idea of "The Andy Griffiths Show," but I can tell you that it is available for free. If watching a few episodes with your child brings you to a discussion of women's rights in the south and how our country has progressed these past 50 years, that conversation suits me just fine.

Speaking of North Carolina, some parents I know up that way felt forced to send their 14-year-old son to treatment for addiction to video games two years ago. Jeremy had refused to do homework, refused to go to school, refused to participate in family activities, refused to eat (not a typo) unless and until he was allowed to play a violent video game six or eight hours every weekday, more on the weekends. After making good progress in wilderness therapy, Jeremy went on to spend a year at a residential treatment facility to do more work on his addiction to video games. He is now enrolled in a traditional boarding school and doing pretty well.

The irony is that Jeremy's parents are allowing Jeremy's brothers— ages 12 and 10—to play video games.

"They'll be ostracized," Jeremy's parents say. "All the kids play video games. They won't have any friends if they don't."

So, I'm reaching out to my community of readers and friends with these questions:

What TV shows do you recommend for 12 year olds?

Are there kids in your neighborhood who don't play video games? Is so, what do these kids do?

And in your home, when do you say, "Enough is enough"?

Some Expert

As long suffering readers will doubtless acknowledge, I am all about making brownies with young children. Making brownies is all about math: if three teaspoons is one tablespoon, how many teaspoons is two tablespoons? Making brownies is all about chemistry: mixtures, combinations, reactions, and--more rarely--explosions. Making brownies is also all about hanging out with the kids, making a mess and making memories, working toward a common, yummy goal.

Making brownies is also about brownies: They're done; they're hot. Let's eat! (The brownies can cool later; let's eat them now!)

So imagine my disappointment, having promised the kids that we were going to make brownies, only to discover that we were out of one of the key ingredients: oil. Not a drop, canola or safflower, in the house.

The children were still in their pajamas and the thought of dealing with organizing them in the car was more than my Saturday morning single-dad brain could cope with. I had been meaning to leave them at home alone for a while (I know this would be a better story if I could remember exactly how old they were) so I determined to dash out to the market, buy some oil, and be back before you can say, "The Department of Children and Families has determined to place your kids in foster care."

So I sped off to the corner grocery store. Obviously, I grabbed a few other necessary food stuffs while I was there Even before adolescence, my kids consumed food like a proverbial biblical plague of locusts. Needless to say, the checkout line stretched into infinity and of course, after waiting frenetically while each and every customer ahead of me counted out pennies and searched pockets for coupons, I was sprinting back across the parking lot to the car before I remembered that I had forgotten to procure the one item I truly needed: as impossible as it seems, in my distracted state I had overlooked to grab a bottle of oil.

Of course now I am faced with two equally impossible alternatives: I can go back in the store, get the oil, wait through the interminable checkout line AGAIN, and watch as my brain oozes out my ears as I go stark raving mad knowing that I have left my little guys home alone for too long. Or I can return home without the oil which, you have to admit, makes no sense either.

Accordingly, I went back into the market and shoplifted.

That's right: David Altshuler, alleged moral exemplar of youth and sententious moralizer about how to model appropriate behavior, stole a bottle of canola oil. Not that I'm making a recommendation mind you, but it was easier than I might have thought. Perhaps if my career as an educational consultant and author doesn't pan out, I can make a living as a petty thief.

The children were fine when I returned home. We made brownies, took the dog for a walk, read some Dr. Seuss, ate some brownies, had a bath, played with Legos, ate some more brownies, thought about having some dinner, and went to bed well before mid-night.

Needless to say, the next day with the children safely in school, I returned to the store and, after trying unsuccessfully to explain what I had done and why--"you stole oil? What?"--just left three dollars on the counter at customer service and walked away. To the best of my knowledge, the three dollars may be there still.

My point is that anyone reading these essays who thinks that the author knows everything about parenting will be sorely disappointed. There are few precepts endorsed in these pages that haven't been disproved in my own experience.

Spend time with your kids and treasure every possible moment. Well, duh. I believe strongly in both "the days are long, but the years fly" and "you're a long time dead." What could be more precious than seeing your kiddoodles covered in flour watching the timer waiting for the brownies to come out of the oven? But I've worked with families where the seagull dad swooped in only rarely to make a lot of noise and poop on everything and the kids turned out fine. So I don't know. I guess the recipe for brownies is much more simple and straightforward than the recipe for offspring.

Parenting might remain more art than science. Go with your gut; believe in yourself; learn from your mistakes; and try not to shoplift more often than is absolutely necessary might remain precepts.

I suspect that if you're reading these chapters that you are making the best decisions you can for your kids with love in your heart and the information available to you in a tough culture.

Good for you.

Here's my last bit of advice for the week: stop reading this book. Put it down. Get off the computer. If your kids are little, go tear up the kitchen and make some brownies. If your kids are grown and gone, give 'em a call and ask them if they remember the time when you tore up the kitchen making brownies.

And in the meantime, make it a point to try not to get arrested.

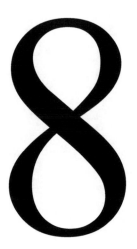

Anger Assessment

I am doing my part to support our on-going work to help one
another be the best people that we can by offering the following
helpful guide to allow you to determine whether or not someone is
angry with you. With these basic Anger Assessment tools at your
disposal, it will be simplicity itself to discern whether or not the
person with whom you are communicating is upset with you. Being
aware of these subtle social cues will help you make better decisions

in your dealings with the folks at work as well as the people in your personal life. The Anger Assessment Index will work with young or old, rich or poor. It is effective with those who are "slow to anger" as well as those who have a quick flash point.

Be on the lookout for these understated but critical indications that someone is cross with you. Although this guide is neither exhaustive nor foolproof, the following first approximation should be of useful. If you notice any of the following signs, you may assume that the person you are speaking with has become dissatisfied with some substantial aspect of your interaction.

1) You perceive words of the form "you stupid son of a bitch" or "why don't you put a gun in your mouth?" directed at you.

2) You notice hands wrapped tightly around your throat with thumbs pointed inward cutting off the airflow to your trachea. Shortness of breath followed by mild nausea and rapid heartbeat ensue. Losing consciousness is an especially cogent indicator.

3) You observe a hand with fingers closed into a formation commonly referred to as a "fist" coming into contact with your nose with sufficient force as to produce copious bleeding from said orifice.

In any of these instances, you may infer that someone is angry with you.

Similarly, here is a sign of a sick culture that is sinking fast: This morning I met a perfect stranger on the street who, within 60 seconds of "Nice day" launched into an endless diatribe about his 11-year-old son's grade point average, SAT scores, extra-curricular activities, and plans for college six years in the future.

Mind you I had not identified myself as a college admissions professional and a quick perusal of my apparel confirmed that nowhere on my tee shirt were the words "tell me how quickly your family is hurtling down the road to nowhere" emblazoned.

It was clear to me that this man who seemed normal and pleasant enough in every other regard, was a hysterical piranha regarding the subject of where his son would go to college. The demons that were stalking his family were all too real to him, the need for constant worry all too immediate.

If random strangers feel the need to justify their curricular choices when I am staggering around the neighborhood on an early morning dog walk, then the collective anxiety level is clearly well past the red zone.

The irony of building your family's psychic home on Anxiety Lane is that children thrive on relaxation, respect, freedom, down-time, and calm more than they respond to pressure, badgering, anxiety, and parents riding off in all directions at once. Pressuring your kids to relax makes as much sense as "Wake up, it's time for your sleeping pill."

The reality is that any loving parent can tell that her child is doing well in school (or not.) C'mon. Do you actually need a report card? You know very well whether your child is reading Vonnegut rather than playing "Shoot, Shoot, Shoot, Blood, Blood, Blood, Kill, Kill, Kill." Do you truly not know whether or not your child loves learning? Is he attuned to the world around him or is he checked out most of the time? Are you content with your child's education or are you stopping random strangers in the middle of their morning dog walks to pontificate and justify the choices you have made for your child?

If you answered yes to any of the rhetorical questions in the paragraph above, then maybe there is a need for my "Guide to Tell if Someone is Actually Angry with You."

Zits Okay!

To promote my previous book, <u>Love the Kid You Get. Get the Kid You Love</u>, I was pleased to be interviewed by Roxy Vargas of "Six in the Mix." I was not nervous about being on television having participated in this medium once before--with Chuck Zinc or, "Skipper Chuck" as he was known in 1961 when precocious children, including my five-year-old unpublished self, appeared on his television show in the geological epoch known to loving parents everywhere as the "Pre-Barney" era. That a flesh and blood human, albeit one wearing a silly boating hat, has been replaced by an enormous purple dinosaur is the subject of another chapter. For now, let me repeat that I wasn't anticipatory or the least bit nervous about BEING ON LIVE TELEVISION IN FRONT OF MILLIONS OF PEOPLE WITHOUT SO MUCH AS A REHEARSAL until, on my way to the studio, thoughtfully located a scant 90-minute nerve wracking drive from my home, I noticed in the rear-view mirror, a zit on my nose.

And not just any zit, mind you. This was a zit of enormous proportions. This zit had its own gravitational field. Were Stephen Hawking to become aware of the existence of this zit, he would rethink his ideas about black holes being the most massive objects in the universe.

It turns out that the Great Wall of China is not, as is commonly believed, visible from space. But I believe orbiting Cosmonauts glancing down at our planet may be traumatized for years to come: First Cosmonaut: "Did you see THAT?"

Second Cosmonaut: "Yes, Comrade! What a big zit!"

As I plodded along on I-95 (aka "The world's longest parking lot") I frequently checked the rear view mirror to see if the cars behind me were moving at more than 10 miles per hour and to ask myself if I were truly a 58 year old man about to be interviewed on live television or, to the contrary, a high school student on the way to his first prom. With his face obscured by a zit the size of Jacksonville.

My monomaniacal nose notwithstanding, the interview went pretty well: I was able to condense three decades of thinking about, reading about, writing about, and working with adolescents and their families into a three-minute Q and A. Perhaps I left out a few of the finer details--theories of development, recent trends in college admissions, the future of therapeutic boarding schools, new research

30

results in the study of addiction treatment, my next book. But you can't have everything. Roxy Vargas and the staff of Channel Six were polite and professional. When Roxy finished my interview, she immediately went on to the next studio to dialogue with the 20-member drum section of a high school marching band. I was too relieved and exhausted to notice whether or not any of the actual adolescents had zits of their own.

What is the take away for loving parents trying to connect with their kids? No, the lesson here is not, "You have a face for radio." The message is that what seemed so important at the time, very likely, wasn't.
Remember how concerned you were about potty training? Remember how all your friends with older children kept telling you that "she won't walk down the aisle in diapers"? Doesn't that seem like a long time ago now? Don't you wish you had been calmer throughout the whole process? Don't you agree that your anxiety only made things worse?

Remember how apprehensive you were when your daughter ended up in the regular math class rather than the class for advanced math students back in sixth grade? Would it even be possible to exaggerate how little difference that divergence of paths has made now that she is an adult? Wouldn't your life have been better if you had been less concerned about which math class your daughter took when she was 11?

Remember how connected you were about the choice of undergraduate institution? Looking back, now that your son is out of college, can you reasonably argue that this choice has turned out to be predictive of his current contentment? Now that your son lives in a different city, don't you wish that you and he had spend more time tossing a ball and less time worrying about which college would admit him?

What might have made a difference in your ultimate relationship with your child was your attitude toward the developmental milestones along the way. We have talked a lot in these chapters about the importance of being there for your kids. I'd like to amend that suggestion to include "not being a hysterical piranha" at the same time.

Unless, of course, you're stuck on I-95 on your way to a live TV interview with a zit the size of the Sahara Desert on your nose. In which case screaming panic is not only allowed but also encouraged.

10

Constructive Criticism

The woman at the 72nd Street pay phone had strands of dirty tinfoil in her matted hair and an enormous collection of broken pieces of plastic in her rusty shopping cart. She turned to show me the enormous ring of keys in her hand, insisting that one of them would fit into the door of the magnificent million-dollar brownstone across the street that she owned but couldn't unlock.

Then, as fast as a flash of lightning across a clear sky, she started haranguing me about my having killed John F. Kennedy. Flecks of spittle punctuated her pointed accusations; she seemed quite convinced that I was responsible and spared no detail in her lengthy diatribe.

Rather than pointing out that I was seven years old at the time of the assassination and not a particularly sophisticated marksman, I decided to find another pay phone and shuffled off through the Upper East Side. The schizophrenic homeless woman returned to the receiver. To this day, I am not certain whether or not she was actually connected to anyone.

Fast-forward thirty years: I'm reviewing case files. I find the following notes and emails:

"I don't know how to thank you for this first success and for having connected with my son."

And

"Ross is happier than a pig in mud; we never would have found _____ College without your patient insight and guidance."

And

"You took the anxiety out of a visceral process. Hannah's friends are all panicked and stressed about getting their applications in but she finished her essays weeks ago and is able to attend to her school work and enjoy her life."

And

"Gus has been clean for three years now; we don't know how to express our gratitude. You have saved our son's life."

But I also found this note:

"Ricky is still using. We haven't heard from him in over a year and have no idea where he is living, presumably on the street somewhere. Following your advice, we spent his entire college fund on treatment and we don't even know if he is alive or dead. Our entire family is in shambles. It is hard to imagine how things could have turned out worse. Thanks for nothing."

Of course I was hurt, devastated really. I had known Ricky his whole life, cared deeply about him and his family. I was deeply saddened at the time when he ran away and was upset that he wasn't sober after three stints in expensive rehab facilities.

And then it dawned on me - the woman with the tinfoil in her hair and the shopping cart was back. She had somehow managed to send me an email and was still channeling messages from her controllers on Neptune. She was still unhappy with my professionalism, my recommendations, and the outcome. She wanted to make sure that her annoyance was expressed and that I got the memo loud and clear. For reasons of her own, she just wanted me to feel bad.

Slow down a sec, I tell myself. That's no way to look at criticism. There's no reason to internalize this misery. Ricky's parents have legitimate concerns. Perhaps there's something for me to learn here. After all, the child didn't get better, is still an active drug user.

Perhaps, indeed. But why do I feel so badly looking at this poor result from a client of years ago? After all, I'm an adult with a graduate degree, three published books, and 30 years of adoring clients who still write me notes thanking me for "changing their lives." Certainly I have enough good will in my self-confidence account to weather the occasional negative comment.

But this chapter is not about adults with professional success. It's about children and teenagers and young adults who are just figuring out who they are and where they fit in the world. And it's about how we - their parents and grandparents and aunts and uncles and teachers and counselors and everyone else who loves them - can best help these precious people both grow into successful adults who can enjoy their young years and feel good about making the best decisions that they can.

Unfortunately, these kids don't have the advantage of a life's worth of psychological callouses to protect them. And as you have likely realized by now, many adults don't have very strong psychic armor either. That's why unnecessary and often untrue comments, barbs, and sarcasm can be so hurtful. And why we have to be ever vigilant to temper our disapproval with our kids.

Truth is, constructive criticism is usually the later and seldom the former. And even when it's delivered with compassion, concern, and consideration it's not always taken that way.

"You got a 96 on your exam? What's the matter? Don't they give hundreds in that school?"
When in doubt, go with unconditional positive regard rather than clever condemnation, no matter how witty.

Who knows? Maybe the critical note was actually trying to help me be a better counselor. Maybe the comments were intended to be motivational, to spur me on to greater heights, to encourage me to study, practice, and hone my skills even further.

Maybe. But regardless of how the message was intended, that's not how it was received. And the great lesson here is that our kids don't always hear what we say the way we want them to either.

Which simply suggests that we should look to be overwhelmingly supportive, loving, and encouraging--even when the voices in our head are telling us otherwise.

36

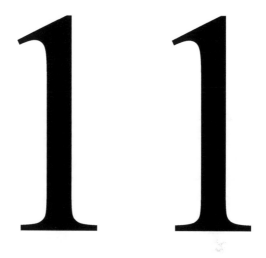

Bear With Me

In June of 1973, eight of my Troop 64 buddies and I hiked a portion of the Appalachian Trail in Western North Carolina for a week. Although the exact locations and distances of this trek are lost to memory, it is no exaggeration to say that the last words we heard from an adult pointing at a map were, "We'll pick you up next Monday at this point here."

The oldest of our group had just turned 18; some of our number were not yet high school graduates. Yet except for the danger or losing our breath from the altitude or the beautiful mountain vistas, there was nothing exceptionally treacherous about a week in the woods. Yes, the trail was muddy because of the summer rain. No, we did not always have dry socks. Yes, Ari Mecklenberg's backpack was eaten by a bear, but no, Ari wasn't wearing his backpack at the time so it could have been worse.

Those of us whose backpacks had not been devoured by a bear gave Ari something to eat and something to wear. I have no subsequent information about whether or not the bear, in addition to eating Ari's backpack, also ate Ari's clothes or the state of the bear's digestive system if he did so. I don't remember Ari bathing much when he wasn't 50 miles from the nearest shower, so maybe the bear got what he deserved if he got a tummy ache from ingesting too many of Ari's sweaty tee-shirts.

In any case, I cannot help but compare teenagers finding their way across mountain trails a generation ago with teenagers today who are not allowed to walk the family dog around the block without a global positioning satellite device and air support. No wonder our kids want to try new things and end up making bad decisions. Our kids haven't had the opportunity to make a bad decision ("Let's go off the trail here and take this short cut which will turn out to add three hours to our hike so we can learn how to make camp in the dark!") so how can they be expected to know how to make a good one? Their every hour and every action is prescribed: "Make a cross court passing shot," "Read 30 pages of this book." Time for reflection is unlikely, time for boredom unheard of.

Which is not to say that I am advocating for letting our adolescents trot off to the wilderness unsupervised to feed their backpacks to the nearest Ursa americanus. But letting children "find their own path" and "follow their own star" are more than just metaphors. Isn't it our anxiety as parents that causes us to encourage our children to have their every hour spoken for? And aren't we losing sight of what we truly want for our kids when we focus on their credentials rather than on their abilities, when we point to their grades on a piece of paper rather than to the knowledge in their heads?

"I have an A in Algebra II, Mr. Altshuler, so I can go to a good college, right?"

"I love math, Percy. Tell me what topic you're enjoying the most."

"Oh, we don't actually learn math in math class. The math teacher is out on maternity leave and the substitute doesn't know any math. So we watch movies with helicopter crashes. But the point is that I have an A in math, right?"

Children need some unstructured time to figure out who they are and what they want. It is more likely that they will assume the responsibility for their own learning and their own process if so.

Because at some point the issue isn't what grades your child has on a piece of paper but the information, ability, and resilience she has in her own head. And wouldn't it be to her advantage if she could find her way from Point A to Point B using only a map and a compass; get along with some other sweaty adolescents; provide food and clothing for the unfortunate Ari Mecklenbergs of our world; and avoid being eaten by a bear?

12

The City Mouse and the Country Mouse

Running with half a dozen buddies in the early morning on New Year's Day, I asked a friend what she and her teen-aged children had done the night before. "Just stayed home and played Parcheesi," Danielle said. "Then the kids and I started to watch a movie, but I fell asleep on the couch in the living room."

"My kids and I stayed home too," I replied. "We played Dominoes and then they baked something that was almost edible. But I'm leaving out the word 'just.' I'm happy to hang out with my wife and children. The kids will be grown and gone soon enough."

As we trotted over tree roots on our way down toward Matheson Hammock, another running buddy joined the conversation: "You supercilious prig," Lynn began. "Not only are you living in a cave, you are harming your kids by not letting them go out from the damp, dark confines in the side of a cliff."

Danielle and I exchanged a glance. It was hard to tell if Lynn was kidding or just exaggerating to make a point. Danielle said, "I didn't force them to stay home or refuse to allow them access to their phones; it's just a tradition. We always hang out as a family on December 31."

Lynn's response was emphatic. "The world isn't happening in your moldy home. Your kids didn't want to be home with you! You have to let your kids out into the broader culture. By denying your children exposure to parties, technology, and every good social advance, you are ensuring that they will be behind the curve socially at college in a few years. Do you think computers are going away? Do you think there are any opportunities for kids who know how to play dominoes rather than how to use electronics? And what's this about not allowing your kids go to parties at the home of friends on New Year's Eve? Are you kidding? The world is happening. Kids have to know how to drink responsibly."

Danielle and I listened thoughtfully as Lynn went on. "Hello, it's 1954 and it wants New Year's Eve back." Danielle and I smiled as we all kept running. "Of course, I smoke pot with my kids," Lynn continued. "How are they going to learn the effect of marijuana if I'm not there to teach them? Wake up and smell the cannabis, you two."

I thought about interrupting and mentioning unequivocal studies concluding that marijuana today is unquestionably addictive and damaging to developing brains, but Lynn kept talking. "News flash. Kids smoke pot. The only question is whether my children are going to smoke pot under my supervision or whether they're going to go out and smoke pot in dangerous circumstances."

Danielle started to say something, but Lynn kept on. "It's not like I let them smoke and drive. After dinner last night, we got a cab and went out to South Beach. It is such a great scene: clubs, music, fashion. So much happening, so much to see. So many great people. We saw one of the Miami Heat players and my son almost got an autograph."

Lynn went on to berate us about how pot is now legal in many states with more coming on board, but I had stopped listening and I think Danielle had too. "Your kids don't even know what they're missing out on," Lynn finished. "Have fun living with the Luddites."

Lynn dropped back to chat with some other runners in our group and Danielle and I plodded along in thoughtful silence. Neither the herons in the bay nor the sun coming up over the horizon seemed overly concerned with the one-sided conversation.

"I wonder why it is so important for Lynn to feel that he's right about smoking pot with his kids," I began. When Danielle didn't answer, I asked her what she was thinking about.

"Oh, nothing really," she said. "Just that when I fell asleep on the couch during the movie, my daughter got a blanket and tucked me in. I'm not sure, but I think she might have given me a kiss on my forehead before she went to bed."

We all want what's best for our kids. We all want to give them the gifts we have. I can't help but wonder which investments will pay the broader dividend down the road. Maybe the child who spent an impaired New Year's Eve on South Beach chasing celebrity autographs will feel connected to and responsible for his aging parents a generation hence.

But my money is on the kid who played board games with his family and gave his mom a kiss on the forehead after tucking her in with a blanket.

13

Over the River and Through the Woods

In 1972, sixteen year-old, Tess arrives from North Jersey to stay with cousins and to visit her Miami grandmother whom she hasn't seen in some years. Rather than call in advance, Tess looks forward to surprising her mom's mom. But when Tess arrives at her grandmother's home, her grandmother looks stricken.

"I didn't know you were coming," she says. "I don't have any food in the house."

"That's fine, Grandma. I came to see you. I'm not hungry."

"You're not hungry? All I have is cottage cheese. If I'd known you were visiting, I would have prepared a nice meal."

The awkwardness is deafening. The conversation never recovers. Tess's grandmother is unable or unwilling to talk about anything other than her surprise and disappointment about not having been informed of the visit. Tess, feeling unwelcome, soon leaves. She does not call her grandmother for the rest of her week in Miami. Nor does her grandmother call her.

On Tess's grandmother's next birthday, Tess does not send a card. On Tess's next birthday, her grandmother does not call. Because of the distance between New Jersey and Miami, it is easy for Tess and her grandmother to avoid one another. They don't show up to the same family functions. Weddings and funerals come and go.

In sum, they do not speak for the rest of the grandmother's life.

How is it possible that members of the same family can allow a slight--real or imagined, big or small, intentional or accidental--to have an effect from which there is no recovery? Was there a history of bad feeling between Tess's cousins and their grandmother? Was there a difference in social class between the two branches of the family? Was there a history involving a surprise visit or a bad meal? Had Tess's grandmother been disappointed when Tess's family had moved from Miami to New Jersey?
Anything is possible. But at the end of the day, either the family stays together or it falls apart.

Thirty years later, Tess, who has been married for twenty years, is getting divorced. Tess is furious with her ex-husband whom she blames for the dissolution. She tells her three children that their father was abusive, a philanderer, and a drunk. She works hard and succeeds in alienating the children from their father. She tells both sides of the extended family, "You're either with me or against me. If you're friends with him, you can't be friends with me." Tess refuses all contact with anyone who stays in touch with her ex.

In the decade since the end of Tess's marriage, two of her three children have had no contact with their father. Their father sends birthday presents to his children; the packages are returned unopened. The oldest of Tess's children is to be married next month. Her father is not invited to the wedding.

***

Experts talk about "splits and cut-offs." They talk about people who are emotionally flooded, who cannot make good decisions because they are overwhelmed. Just like it can be hard to hear in a crowded room, it can be hard to focus on what is in the best interests of your children when your own all-consuming anger prevents you from "hearing" their needs. No matter how hurt and angry you are, it is seldom in a child's interest to be turned against and have no contact with a parent. Surely your love of your child is greater than your hatred for her other parent.

Experts also talk about "modeling," about how apple trees seldom produce pears.

Could the incident with the surprise visit all those years ago have "caused" Tess to be so completely and thoroughly vicious to her husband a generation later? Of course that explanation seems too simplistic. There are a host of other factors at play in any family.

And maybe Tess's husband was abusive, a philanderer, and a drunk. Maybe the only way for Tess to get away from him was to cut off all contact. Maybe her children were at risk.

Maybe.

But as an actual member of Tess's family, I am here to tell you that by any objective measure, her husband was none of those things. He might have spent too much time trying to make his law practice successful; he might not have changed as many diapers as Tess would have liked. But he was a loving, decent guy who did the best he could. It is a crime that he did not get to watch his children grow up.

It was not in the children's interests to have their father ripped from their lives. It's a shame for a dad to miss a child's soccer game. It's a crime for a dad to miss a child's wedding. How will this next generation resolve conflict? How will Tess's kids ever learn to say the magic words, "Okay, I guess we disagree but we have to move forward as a family"?

The point is, if there is someone is your family to whom you haven't spoken for some time, it might be in your children's interest for you to pick up the phone.

14

You Can Do It

If my gracious readers can accept yet another marathon analogy, I respectfully ask them to plod through the initial sentences of this post; I promise to make a point about your children and your children's education. Eventually. First though, join me for a thought experiment regarding that deep-seated, enduring foolishness that occurs at Mile 20 both on the course and next to it.

With six miles to go, many runners are internalizing the truism that "the race begins now." Their bodies, having used up their allotment of glycogen and good sense, are "running on empty", hoping to achieve by force of will what is no longer physiologically likely. Some are on the way to a transplendent celebration of the human spirit and a well-deserved banquet of food and congratulations; some are on the way to the medical tent with spikey fevers and IV glucose solutions.

Consider the spectators cheering their lungs out and waving those wonderful, hand-made signs. "You can do it!" "You got this!" "Pain is fatigue leaving the body!" It is hard to imagine anything more fun except for the posters that go beyond simple encouragement to wickedly clever: "Run like you stole something!" "I hear there is bacon at the finish line. Hurry!" And my favorite, "Great job, random stranger!"

"Pain is temporary; pride is forever" is inspiring for those runners for whom the finish line is attainable, for those who have to suck it up, guts it out, and overcome a couple more clichés to stagger bloody but unbowed to the finish line.

But what about those who can't make it? What about those participants who, at Mile 20, are no longer runners, but staggerers? What about the competitors who are prostrate on the asphalt, their hamstrings twitching uncontrollably, their bodies shut down? Will even the hilarity of the placard proclaiming, "You think this is tough? Try growing out bangs" be enough to get them up and running again?

Of course not. Even "Beast mode" painted in day-glow colors does nothing for an insentient runner.

Does the runner sprawled convulsing on the sidewalk not KNOW that the finish line is six miles that way? Is there some INFORMATION that would be helpful? Perhaps the runner didn't hydrate properly, maybe the runner didn't train perfectly, maybe--as is frequently the case--the runner ran the first 20 miles too fast.

But at this point in shutdown mode, it just doesn't matter. There is nothing anyone can do or say to get the runner up and going. Maybe he can guts it out and limp the last ten kilometers, but running at the pace of the previous 20 miles is out of the question. No amount of "You can do this!" is going to matter.

Now imagine an 11th grade student who has failed second year algebra for the second time. Tommy has been to see his patient teacher for extra help; he has attended every review session; he has patiently done homework and worked assiduously with a private tutor. Yet his exams results remain lower than the proverbial snake's belly in a wagon rut.

The asymptotes of the hyperbola ($y = +/-$ a/b x, as you doubtless remember) are still Sanskrit. He just isn't getting it. Maybe Tommy has learning differences. Maybe he has issues with spatial reasoning. Maybe he shouldn't be in algebra II because of his poor background in algebra I. What is to be done?

Well, you could try yelling at him. That's what many misguided parents do. You could make placards and hold them up while Tommy studies. "May the course be with you" becomes even cleverer when applied to math classes rather than the roads from Hopkinton to Boston. You could be supportive; you could be punitive; indeed, you could stand on your head for all the difference it would make. The fact of the matter is not everyone can get though algebra II just like not everyone can run through all five boroughs of NY.

The tricky bit of course is that the direction of the causal arrow gets reversed. Just like runners twitching on the sidewalk have been known to be ungracious even to the most thoughtful care providers, kids who are berated, poked, prodded, "motivated," and insulted about their performance in math can be miserable to live with. Failing kids can be snarky and turn to prevaricating: "We don't have any homework;" "I got an A on my test."

And who could blame them?

When your child doesn't perform, consider "can't" rather than "won't" as an explanation. And it's not that he needs more

50

information either. Telling a student "your mother and I expect you to do well in math class" is as helpful as telling a runner with a broken leg that "the finish line is that way." Really? Is there any doubt in your mind that your child doesn't KNOW you expect him to get good grades?

Nobody ever woke up in the morning and said, "I know what I'll do: I'll flunk math to annoy my parents" any more than anyone ever lined up in the dark 26.2 miles from somewhere thinking "it would really bother the people who care about me if I start convulsing and barfing six miles from the end of this race."

Thinking "can't" rather than "won't" is the first step toward finding a workable solution.

15

Avoiding False Choices

I would prefer that my children read Cicero, Vergil, Ovid, and Horace in the original Latin rather than in English translations. The advantages of knowing ancient languages are legendary: insight into sentence structure, awareness of parts of speech, and understanding of the roots of modern languages. Kids who learn Latin achieve a sense of mastery. In short, Latin beats English, manus down.

The problem is that my kids don't know Latin. So I can yell at them, threaten them, berate them, and punish them waiting for them to become fluent. Or I can encourage them to read the Aeneid in translation. Insisting that students read ancient languages rather than translations completely misses the point. It's a false choice.

I would rather my child sit still in class, take notes, attend to her ninth grade science teacher, and perform well on each written evaluation. This tried and true paradigm of learning is preferable to what she currently does which is sit in her teacher's swivel chair occasionally bouncing and rolling.

Sitting still she learns nothing. Moving around a bit allows her to understand everything. The choice isn't sit still versus move around; the choice is move around or not learn. If you are a kid who can sit still in a traditional classroom and learn, more power to you. I admire your ability to focus on the lecture, take accurate notes, and perform well on exams. If, on the other hand, you are a kid who needs to move around a bit in order to concentrate, I hope you will have the opportunity to have your needs met.

I would prefer that my daughter's science fair project involve "Analytic and algebraic topology of locally Euclidean parameterization of infinitely differentiable Riemannian manifolds" rather than "Our Friend the Beaver."*

Ignoring for a moment the vast majority of science fair projects undertaken and completed by parents in which the children take no active part, I will suggest that children seldom choose between these two topics. It's the animal-in which the child is interested and can write eloquently-or cheating, disappointment, and failure when she is thrown into a topic with which few of us would be comfortable.

I would rather my child attend Princeton University and be successful rather than have her enroll at North Cornstalk State Drooling College and do well.

Agreed.

However, positive outcomes at Princeton versus success in the classroom at NCSDC is a false choice. The actual alternatives are matriculating at North Cornstalk or sitting around forever feeling bad about not going to New Jersey.
The lesson "accept your children for who they are rather than for who you want them to be" is clear. Loving your kids for who they are is the only real choice.

* I am indebted to Tom Lehrer for the first title and to Gary Trudeau for the second.

16

Questions of Privacy

I am the first to admit that perhaps I take privacy a tad too seriously. In the sense that possibly Noah was willing to acknowledge that he had seen enough rain. I live in a big city where "stranger danger" is all too real, so I taught all four of my children to be vary of adults asking personal questions. Under any circumstances. Ever. "People who need to know where we live already know where we live!" I intoned endlessly. "Anyone who asks you where you go to school doesn't need to know where you go to school!"

My delicate concern--"paranoia" is such a value laden word--about privacy was badgered yet again on a recent tour of Eastern Massachusetts boarding schools when a colleague asked our student guide a personal question.

My fellow counselors and I had already seen the admissions office, the soccer fields, the indoor swimming pool, the ice hockey rink, the cafeteria, a dorm room, the student union, the robotics lab, the chapel, and more classrooms than I could remember or distinguish. A dozen of us were now following our tour guide across the quad toward the stables.

Like a car careening through an intersection, one of my fellow counselors asked our tour guide, "Are you Episcopal?" I cringed. Surely this young man's religious convictions were a matter between him and his family or him and his God (or lack of one.) How could our understanding of his school be enhanced by my knowing which church he attended? Awkward! I winced, embarrassed to the core.

The joke was on me as it turned out in that the questioner was referring to the school in general not the young man in particular. "You" was second person plural, not second person singular. Neither the 17-year-old student nor the 170-year-old school had an overwhelming religious affiliation as it happened. "Episcopal lite" I dutifully recorded in my notebook. "Religion of tour guide thankfully undisclosed."

But within minutes, I once again observed my colleagues asking questions that can only be considered boundary crossing, intrusive, and--shame on us-- offensive. Subsequent to the dreaded religion question, my colleague asked our intrepid guide, "Where are you applying to college?"

Maybe I'm over sensitive--look, I admitted I might be over sensitive in the first paragraph, okay?--but this question annoys me like people taking phone calls in a movie theater. Surely these youngsters are not cuts of meat wrapped in cellophane in a market to be examined and prodded, purchased or put back. Why do we need to know the specifics of this youngster's transition process? Doesn't he have enough stress with supplemental essay questions and early action deadlines? Isn't choosing and applying to college enough of a nightmare without the added humiliation of public disclosure?

Because what if the answers were of the sort that no reasonable young adult would care to reveal? "I flunked algebra; I have to go to the local community college;" "My dad is a gambling addict so there are no funds available for college;" "I just got out of wilderness therapy. I have to attend a step-down program to complete treatment for my depression, substance abuse, and self-harm." How dare we ask questions the answers to which are none of our business?

If you were a first-time guest in my home, would you have the temerity to ask me "What is your annual pre-tax income?" or "How many times did you and your wife 'go to the movies' last year?" Certainly not. You would be handed your coats before the soup course whether or not you winked when you said "movies".

Why do we as adults feel free to subject strangers to such personal questions, just because they are showing us around their boarding school homes but can't yet vote?

Obviously, the rules are different in our offices where we, as educational consultants, are required to inquire about personal information. I can't recommend appropriate schools to a client without knowing her grades, test scores, extra-curriculars, learning style, financial situation, and yes, maybe even religious beliefs. But our tour guides had signed no wavers. We were guests in their homes. Why do we feel no compunction about poking about in their academic and emotional cupboards?

At the very least, shouldn't we preface our questions with disclaimers? "You know you don't have to answer this, but could you tell me a little bit about what you might change at this school if you could?" "Stop me if I'm crossing a boundary, but would you feel comfortable sharing where you are applying to college?"

Every school has summary data of where their seniors are heading next fall. "Of our one hundred graduates last year, five will be matriculating at Princeton and four will be enrolling at North Cornstalk University." This information tells us everything we need to know to factor in whether or not the school might be an appropriate fit for a client. Using our positions of authority as consultants and adults to scrutinize specific disclosures impresses me as shameful and a tad voyeuristic. Instead, let's use our position of leadership to model appropriate boundaries. I for one will feel less awkward as I tour with my respected colleagues. I think the children will be grateful not to be treated as cuts of beef as well.

17

Winning Argument

"The frying pan was given to us by the Stewart <u>family</u>" replied Mrs. Edwards icily.

"No. It. Wasn't." Mr. Edwards said stopping after each word as if it were a live grenade. "Tommy Stewart was my friend before we got married. You never even met him until after we got engaged."

"Are you kidding? Do I have to sit here and listen to these calumnies?" Mrs. Edwards looked imploringly at her forensic accountant, her attorney, and the mediator. "You know very well that Melissa Stewart and I met in grad school."

"And who paid for your graduate degree?" may I ask.

"I paid you back every cent of those funds and you know it!"

"Not a syllable of truth," said Mr. Edwards. "I have a copy of your journal entry from 1988 in which you clearly state that you didn't like Missy at all."

"A journal entry? What were you doing looking at my journal?" Mrs. Edwards sputtered.

"The same thing you were doing when you were reading my emails without my knowledge or permission!"

"Which is how I found out about that floozy you were seeing."

"How many times do we have to do over this?" Mr. Edwards shouted. "I have told you repeatedly that Tiffany and I didn't start dating until after you had hired this divorce attorney."

"That frying pan was given to me by my friend and I'm not going to let you run off with it like you have with everything else we ever tried to..."

Mr. Edwards interrupted: "If you hadn't turned the children against me, I wouldn't..."

Mrs. Edwards interrupted more loudly: "If you hadn't hidden our assets with the intention of stealing..."

And off they go. I have too much affection for my gentle readers to subject them to any more of this endlessly vapid argument. But I will ask your indulgence with the following middle school level arithmetic question: If the attorneys each charge $450/hour and the forensic accountants each charge $300/hour and the mediator also charges $300/hour, how many minutes can Mr. and Mrs. Edwards talk about the stupid frying pan that couldn't have cost more than $120 to begin with before it would have made more sense to just take a darn cab to Crate and Frigging Barrel to get another one? Clearly, there is something else going on in this room. You don't need a master's degree in marriage and family counseling to notice that Mr. and Mrs. Edwards have some unfinished business to work through. Wouldn't you agree that the frying pan--which is a big lose if they spend more than four minutes talking about it--is the least of their issues?

The real question is not "why are they still fighting?" The question is whether or not the frying pan is worth fighting over.

It seems that Mr. and Mrs. Edwards are "invested" in continuing to fight. They must be "getting something" out of their endless billable meetings with their attorneys and their forensic accountants because they are certainly not obtaining any frying pans.

Which brings us--"finally" you might say--to conversations with our beloved children. What are you spending much of your day talking about with your kids? Is homework a frequent topic? What about chores? Bedtime?

I'm not advocating for abnegating our sacred responsibilities as parents to model appropriate behaviors and to live together in a cooperative household where everyone works and everyone eats. There is no more appropriate parental sentence than "Give me a hand with these dishes and then let's go toss the ball." But if you hear yourself saying, "I have asked you a hundred times to do the dishes! Yesterday you promised you would do the dishes! Why don't you ever do the dishes? Your father didn't do his share of the dished, that's why I divorced him!" then you might be in "Edwards territory".

And something went horribly wrong somewhere way before the attorneys, the forensic accountants, the mediator and the frying pan worth--at most--four minutes of everyone's time.

18

Arithmetic Question

You can skip all the arithmetic and still get the point about how to help your kids grow up happy and healthy. If numbers are not your thing, you can start reading this when you see this symbol, ❖.
For those of you who do believe that "numbers are your friends; you can count on them!" here's a question: "What is the smallest power of 2 that has a "7" in the thousands digit?"

Let's think this through. Go ahead, get a pencil. Heck, get a calculator if you prefer. Whatever you like. Let me help:

Two to the first power is two.

$2^1 = 2$

Two to the second power is four.

$2^2 = 4$

Two to the third power is eight.
$2^3 = 8$
Note that none of these numbers, 2, 4, or 8 even HAS a thousands digit never mind a 7 in the thousands digit. You have to go waaay up the line to get powers of two that have thousands digits:

2, 4, 8, 16, 32, 64, 128, 256, 512, 1024

$2^{10} = 1024$

Now we have a thousands digit, but the number in the thousands digit is a 1. So we have to keep going to get a seven in the thousands digit. Onward and upward:

$2^{11} = 2048$
$2^{12} = 4096$
$2^{13} = 8192$
$2^{14} = 16,384$

$2^{15} = 32,768$ (Ooh, there's a seven. But it's in the hundreds not the thousands place.)

$2^{16} = 65,536$
$2^{17} = 131,072$
$2^{18} = 262,144$

64

$2^{19} = 524,288$
$2^{20} = 1,048,576$
$2^{21} = 2,097,152$

❖(For those readers who are just joining us, welcome back!)

So there you are, the first power of two that has a seven in the thousands digit is 2^{21} or 2,097,152.

Who cares? Well might you ask. Really, nobody. No mathematician cares. Neither Monte Hall nor Alec Trebek is going to ask a question that is this time-consuming to solve without a calculator. There's nothing remotely interesting about arithmetic questions of this type. And no, there are no "short cuts," no "tricks" that will allow this answer to appear without slogging through all those powers of two. The only way to find the first seven in the thousands digit is to go through the steps above using a pencil or a calculator.

Unless, of course, you happen to <u>be</u> a human calculator.

The only aspect of this question that is of interest is "What about the guy who can answer this question "What is the smallest power of 2 that has a "7" in the thousands digit?" without a pencil, without a calculator? What about the guy who answers this question as quickly as you or I could answer, "What is three times five?"

John von Neumann was said to have instantly answered this question about the powers of two. By all accounts von Neumann was indeed a human calculator and could multiply four digit numbers in his head. When he wasn't working on the Manhattan Project or inventing game theory or driving too fast on the streets of Princeton.
Would you agree that von Neumann's "math brain" was different from yours or mine?

Which brings us--'finally' you might say--to my point about raising healthy kids. Remember, the folks who are going to pick out your nursing home are the same folks to whom you may currently be saying, "Why don't you have an 'A' in math?"

Doubtless your child's math course does not involve questions similar to "What is the smallest power of 2 that has a '7' in the thousands digit?" And doubtless you believe that your child could be doing better. "If only she would study harder," you opine. "I'm sure she could get an 'A' if she just worked at it."

Here's a thought experiment: How long would you need to be locked in a sparsely furnished room under a bare light bulb before you could come up with "2,097,152" as the answer to "What is the smallest power of 2 that has a '7' in the thousands digit?" You would argue that you *can't* do that calculation in your head. If someone were to tell you that you're refusing to do that arithmetic or that you "just aren't motivated" or that "you're just getting back at your parents and that's why you won't figure out "What is the smallest power of 2 that has a "7" in the thousands digit?" you would be justifiably and righteously annoyed.

You don't have the arithmetic ability; you don't have the memory; you don't have the motivation. You just plain can't figure out this problem. And if you could figure it out, you darn sure couldn't figure it out instantaneously like von Neumann did.

Which is why you may be having trouble with your child and her math course.

Because in all likelihood she is trying the best she can. The "noise" that is destroying the "signal" is that her annoying behaviors and seeming lack of motivation have been caused by her not being able to do that which she is asked. If she could handle the curriculum, she would.

Just like if you knew "What is the smallest power of 2 that has a "7" in the thousands digit?" you would have said so.

19

Wait for It

In 1981 I purchased my first home, an 1100-square foot, two-bedroom house with jalousie windows and a wall unit air conditioner. Purchase price: $81,000. The mortgage--principle, interest, taxes, and insurance--came to $803/month. Having earned $780/month as a middle school math teacher the year before, I was concerned about my ability to keep up with the payments. So, in addition to tutoring six days a week, I picked up a few shifts at the

68

book store and sold hotdogs at the Orange Bowl during football season. I also taught on Saturdays at the community college, a three-hour, early morning, marathon remedial math class. It would be difficult to exaggerate either how sweet those students were or how unprepared for college work. I will admit that after the second consecutive hour of pontificating about how to find the area of a rectangle of length eight and width six, I was ready for a cool beverage. So I would walk to a delicatessen downtown and indulge in the only pampering I allowed myself in those splendid economic times: I bought a turkey sandwich and a root beer. It was glorious. Even after all these years.

Of course, my story of youthful hardship hardly qualifies. I was blessed with generous parents, an expensive education, and absurdly good health. I never missed a meal and, had I gotten into any kind of financial kerfuffle, there were any number of folks to whom I could have turned for a short-term loan. My point this week is not about political economy nor public policy-topics about which I know nothing. Indeed, Sgt. Schultz knows more about these subjects than I. Nor do I know anything about why any sane institution would front tens of thousands of dollars to a 22-year-old with a credit history composed primarily of empty pizza boxes. I just want to point out how much more appreciative your kids will be if you will stop giving them everything.

Some examples may serve to make the point:

Do you walk into the hall 45 minutes into Beethoven's ninth symphony, trampling over the feet of seated concert goers? Do you chat loudly with your companions pontificating about how the first three movements of opus 125 are just so boring, that only the chorale is worth listening to?

Do you read the last page of the mystery first then, since you already know 'whodunit', do you toss the book aside unread?

Do you always eat dessert first? (And if so, are you apprehensive about health concerns relating to obesity?)

Of course not. Every adult understands the importance of waiting. "Foreplay later" is not a popular long-term plan.

Then why are you denying your children the deep and lasting satisfaction of working hard to achieve a long-term goal? Why do you keep giving them stuff, stuff that they neither appreciate nor enjoy?

No 16 year-old needs a new car. Not unless she has worked outside the home to earn a percentage of the purchase price. The gift of a new car isn't a gift; it's an insult. A new car for a high school kid communicates helplessness on the part of the recipient. That's why, after receiving a $40,000 Lexus, she pitched a boogie crying about how she wanted the BMW.

What's wrong with this picture? Everything.

Even water tastes better after a child has worked up a sweat mowing the lawn.

Remember those snarky, obnoxious, fussy kids whining their way through Disney World the last time you visited Mouse World? You remember those children: they were outraged that they only had seven lollipops when they wanted eight.

Had they paid ten percent of the admission fee, there would have been fewer tears.

Give your children the gift of hard work and accomplishment. Just be prepared for them to still be talking about a turkey sandwich and a root beer 35 years later.

20

Who Are You?

Our frothing ball-of-fluff terrier mix is dedicated to ridding the neighborhood of evil squirrels. On our early morning sojourns while my buddies and I huff and pant, Langley charges ahead, a squirrel seeking missile, a blinding streak of speeding fury. The squirrels ignore his slathering charge, blithely squatting. When Langley is inches away from squirrel implosion, the squirrel throws a hip fake and bounds calmly to the safety of the nearest palm tree.

Undeterred, Langley sets his sights on the next sciurinae sciruus as my running buddies and I plod along chatting about optimism and whether or not dogs have imaginations and if so, what squirrel stew looks like in the mind of a canine.

What also intrigues me is the relative speed of the animals, dog and squirrel. In the straight-away, the squirrel tops out at 12 miles per hour whereas Langley can hit 30 mph with one paw tied behind his back. In a mile run down Fifth Avenue, Langley has finished the race and is headed back to the hotel for a shower when the squirrel hasn't made it half way. The slowest dog is faster than the fastest squirrel.

Then why hasn't Langley ever come close to catching and devouring a squirrel? Because a squirrel has a lower center of gravity, because a squirrel can MOVE side to side before you can blink, because a squirrel knows it's a squirrel and knows what its strengths are. Because a squirrel knows better than to run on a straight course against a dog.

In my professional practice these last 30 years, I see a lot of parents trying to force their squirrel children to be dogs.

Or as Wallace Stegner said, "You can't make a sprinter out of a 250-pound hammer-thrower or a musician out of someone who is tone deaf."

Those of you dear readers who are accountants, imagine the wretchedness of your life had your parents forced you to be trumpet players. Those of you who are trumpet players, try to envision going to work as an accountant.

I have been following my students for over 30 years now. Not one of them has ever said to me, "I wanted to grow up to be an investment banker, but thank the good lord, my mom forced me to be a film-maker."

The fundamental psychic insult is to be told to be someone who you are not, to hear the message repeatedly that you are not okay as you are.

Our job as loving parents is to provide opportunity, to present options, to gently guide our beloved children in the direction toward which they have the most aptitude and affection.
And then to shut up.

Because you can tell your trumpet player all day long to be an accountant, but it's just not what he was meant to do.

Stated another way, even if you could make a silk purse out of a sow's ear, you would still have one unhappy pig.

You never see gay parents trying to convince their heterosexual children to be gay. You know why not? Because they know better. We are who we are. Every ability with which we are born is a gift, not a limitation. But don't tell me that you could be a math professor if you just put your mind to it. If you were meant to be a professor of mathematics, you would already be one.

Wallace Stegner again: "[Writing] is a function of gift-that which is given and not acquired. All any teacher can do is work with what is given."

David Altshuler again: most of the unhappiness I see in my professional practice is caused by loving parents trying to make their kids into that which they are not.

Stated another way, if you make your squirrel run in a straight line, he is going to be caught, killed, and eaten by a dog.

21

Could It Be This Simple?

One of my running buddies has had the unmitigated temerity to suggest that my parenting philosophy can be summed up in the simplistic phrase, "Take your kids camping." So I feel it is high time to amend my advice-honed over 30 years of counseling families-by adding another phrase: "Take your kids hiking too."

Of course my critical running buddy would have to be one of the most respected psychologists in the Southeastern United States. He writes books, gives lectures, serves on panels, and was president of his professional association. Charles knows Freudian psychodynamics like the back of his hand and, unlike this author, can tell you the difference between Carl Jung, Alfred Adler and Otto Rank without having to go to Wikipedia. Charles has as many letters <u>after</u> his name as I have letters <u>in</u> my name. So I listen when he says that good parenting can't be as straight forward as just going hiking and camping with the kids.

Still, I wasn't thinking about Charles at all on a recent, chilly February when my kids and I and some other parents and their kids came to a river, the same river we felt strongly that we had crossed twice previously in the past hour as we zigged and zagged our way up a--and I use the term loosely--"trail". We had been repeatedly "canyoned out", that is to say the slot canyon became particularly slotty, impassable actually.

With no way up and over, we had taken off our shoes and sprinted through the 15 inches of frigid water across the 12-foot stream. But this time we wanted to keep our feet dry and remain on speaking terms with our toes who, we felt certain, might mutiny at any time.

So we built a make-shift "bridge." The kids grabbed fallen trees and threw them across the stream. Ten logs and ten minutes later, we were able to cross the river like Flying Walendas, our toes snug, dry, and warm in our cozy shoes. As great construction projects go, the pyramid at Giza has nothing to worry about.

Nobody said anything about our structure. There was nothing that needed to be said. But look at what was communicated without words: "That's my dad," the kids think. "He's the guy who solves problems with me; he's the guy who trusts me to come up with solutions; he's the guy who would rather be hiking with me than in his office or on his phone; my dad is the guy who gives me a hand

and pulls me up on shore." And for the kid who slipped off our makeshift edifice and got wet up to his knees: "that's the guy who helps me get the dirt out from between my toes then gives me his dry socks when my feel are cold."

Are your kids thinking something else? Instead of the above, are they thinking, "That's my dad. That's the guy who is always telling me to do my homework. That's the guy who would rather return an email than take me hiking in the slot canyons by the river."

Dashill Hamnett has Sydney Greenstreet get it right portraying the villainous Casper Gutman in "The Maltese Falcon." Gutman has promised Humphery Bogart $25,000 (maybe a quarter million in today's dollars) for the stolen, jewel-encrusted statue. But Gutman hands the hardened detective only ten thousand dollars instead.

Sam Spade: We were talkin' about a lot more money than this.

Casper Gutman: Yes, sir, we were. But this is genuine coin of the realm. With a dollar of this you can buy ten of talk.

You can talk all you want about how much you love your kids, how you would do anything for them, how they are the most important thing in the world to you. But it's one thing to talk the talk. It's another thing altogether to hike the hike and give your dry socks to your kid with wet feet.

It would be naïve to suggest that psychological interventions are never necessary and that the only secret of bringing up contented children who get along with their parents and do well in school is to take them for walks in the woods. Maybe over the next 30 years of my professional practice, I will add another sentence to "Take your kids camping; take your kids on a hike." In the meantime, I'm going to ask my buddy Charles how many of the kids he sees in his office spent a lot of time camping and hiking with their parents.

My guess is that the more parents and kids build bridges both actual and metaphorical, the more likely they are to be able to communicate effectively together.

22

Put On A Happy Face

At the gym the other day, I overheard a conversation between two acquaintances who had, by their own objective assessment, the worst most miserable lives ever in the history of the planet Earth from the Australopithecines to the present day. Ungrateful children, galloping health concerns, economic problems of epic proportions, and unmitigated wretchedness from their respective ex-spouses were the least of it. The world had done them wrong and they were intent

78

of letting anyone within earshot know the grim particulars. They "one upped" each other with morbid consistency:

My second ex-wife is taking the kids on a cruise the very weekend I'm having an unpleasant outpatient procedure."

"Oh, yeah? My ex spoils the kids rotten then sends me the invoices. Meanwhile, my attorney's bill has topped what Imelda Marcos spent on shoes."

"Ha! Wait till I tell you about why my idiot of an ex-boss fired me for no reason. Her expectations were ridiculous, completely unfair-- not that she ever explained what they actually were."

"Your ex-husband is three months behind on his child support? That's nothing. Let me tell you..."
Invited to join the conversation, I admitted that things were going pretty well in my world. None of my four children is in the emergency room, my elderly parents enjoy relatively good health, and we have a fridge full of food. No, we don't have any trouble walking around our home for fear of tripping over garbage bags filled with hundred dollar bills, but we get by.

Had I slapped these two with a large fish they could not have been more put off or annoyed by my positive response. They lit into me as if I had stolen their seed corn. How dare I? They were offended that I didn't join the complaint fest. For an instant, I almost felt responsible and believed I should pay their mortgages and take responsibility for hiring someone to kidnap their ex-spouses.

Misery may love company, but in future I'll be looking for less vocally miserable companions. I'm going to chat with folks whose glasses are half full and spare myself the unrelenting downer of these two sad sacks.

Which brings us to my gentle guidance for loving parents for this week: It might be a good idea going forward to model doing the best you can with what you've got.

Students don't learn biology by osmosis; putting the textbook underneath their pillow the night before an exam doesn't bring good grades. Your kids do learn your beliefs by absorbing your every gesture, thought, and expression. Your children are certified alien mind readers when it comes to knowing how you think and what you believe. If you model strength, your kids will be able to display weakness. If you refrain from incessant complaining, your children are more likely to stop grousing as well. They'll know that you have the emotional strength and stability to support them if the seas of their lives ever do actually get rough.

And let's face it: you have less to complain about than any generation in history. Henry the VIII, who owned a large fraction of Europe, would have given half his kingdom for that which you take for granted. When your kids step on a rusty nail, they get a shot of antibiotics and skip home from the pediatrician's office; when Henry's kids stepped on a rusty nail, they got tetanus and dead.

You're complaining about the twenty-dollar co-pay?

Of course parents displaying honest emotion is healthy for kids. There's nothing wrong with acknowledging occasional sadness or displaying tears at a funeral. But an unmitigated outpouring of constant dissatisfaction communicates that the world is an unsafe, unpleasant, overwhelming place. Surely we want our children to have a firmer foundation than believing that every step is bad and about to get worse.

Giving your kids the foundation of "We're doing the best we can with what we've got" and "We have our health and we have each other" will allow and encourage them to have contented lives themselves.

23

I Just Don't Get It

Maybe you can help, gentle readers, with the following folks and their very real problems:

1) Why can't my wife be more understanding? Sure, I have extra-marital affairs. I travel a lot. I have a few different women I see in each city I visit. What does that have to do with my wife? She has

the three young children to take care of. What does she care what I do when I'm out of town?

Okay, so maybe I brought home an STD and she caught it. But I apologized. What else am I supposed to do? And I paid for a good doctor for her to go to. What more does she want? I make a good living. Isn't that enough? Why can't she understand that I just like women and that I want to have sex with as many of them as possible?

2) Why won't my six-year-old read more books? We have lots of books in the house. My husband and I even went on-line to buy "age-appropriate" books, whatever those are. Sure we let our son play "League of Legends" on his Ipad. Of course we let him watch whatever videos he wants whenever he wants on the same device. Yes, he plays on the iPad every minute of every day. But wouldn't you think he'd get tired of all those electronics and want to learn how to read?
His stupid first grade teacher told us the other day that the only way we could get Percy to learn to read would be to take away the device and the video games. Is she crazy? Does she know what it's like to live with this kid when he doesn't get to play on his iPad? He fusses like you wouldn't believe.

Still, I followed her absurd advice. I took away the device just the other day. Percy refused to go to bed. It was after 11:00 at night and he had to be up the next day for school. So I took away the iPad and made him go to bed. I held my ground: "No, you cannot 'just finish one more level'" I said.

But then the next morning when he woke up, he just wanted to play the game some more. So of course I let him. Otherwise, he wouldn't eat his breakfast. And we all know that breakfast is the most important meal of the day. Anyway, he was without his device for almost eight hours--practically the whole time he was asleep. I took away the game just like the teacher said. But it didn't seem to help.

He still wants to play violent video games on the iPad all day. He still doesn't want to learn how to read.

***

Ah, if it were only so simple. If only our own issues with our own families were as obvious and straightforward as those of the two speakers above.

At the risk of explaining the joke, I cannot help but point out how unlikely it is that the man in the first scenario is going to have a committed, meaningful, fulfilling relationship with his wife. Not while he's carrying on with all those other women in all those other towns. An apology about transmitting an STD just isn't going to cut it. Similarly, the mother in the second example is not going to bring up a child who loves reading and loves learning if she gives in to the terrorist demanding that he suckle on screens hour after hour day after day. Taking away the device while the child sleeps doesn't begin to address the issue.

My concern about our ability to bring up children who love to read is a common theme in these chapters. We have no longitudinal research about the cognitive capability of 50-somethings who endlessly played violent video games as children because there were no violent video games when we were children. But what about the broader point of folks who are "living a lie," doing that which is obviously contrary to the interests of their children?

And what about you? And what about me? Is there something in our lives as parents that is so glaringly, blatantly, screechingly obvious that everyone sees it except us?

"I don't know who discovered water, but it wasn't a fish." I don't know about you, but I'm going to be on the lookout for water. If there is something that I'm doing wrong with my kids I'm going to think about it in an intentional way, try to find out what it is, and correct it. In the meantime, I'm going to make sure that the number of my extramarital affairs remains equal to the number of hours I allow my young children to play violent video games.

24

Meet The New Scam

Remember that kid who invented all those brilliant ways to cheat in high school? Even before electronic communications, he was making crib sheets in ingenious ways. Writing information on his sleeve, hiding notes in his sneakers, there was nothing he wouldn't do.

Except study, of course.

Parents today have stolen a page from the playbook of our young fraud. If headlines are to be believed, these misguided folks are now shelling out tens or even hundreds of thousands of dollars to hucksters who profess to have the formula for admissions to top colleges.

What is a top college according to the silliness? One that is high in the rankings of that absurd and--on my street--largely discredited magazine. Fallacy tottering on fallacy. By this logic, why not rank women (or men) from most to least desirable? Ignoring individual differences would allow us all to double the money we spend on a college education and pursue the same people.

For every thousand dollars these parents spend gaming the college admissions process, they should instead take their kids camping (or for a walk on the beach or to the library or to the scrap-booking store or to the home of an elderly neighbor to drop off some home-made cookies.) The investment will pay off in every more meaningful way.

Because the research is unequivocal: who you are matters more than where you go. Kids with ability, whether they go to colleges that admit 6% or 60% of their applicants, end up the same; they do fine independent of the name on the sweatshirt. Kids without ability don't do well. Again, it doesn't matter nearly as much where they go to school.

Of course "ability" is a hard deer to hunt, a tricky term to define. But in this context ability might be defined as "knowing that the test is next Monday, but that there is a paper due next Tuesday and that putting off starting the paper until after the exam will leave only one day to write it which isn't enough so I better shut down the text function on my phone and make an appointment to see the professor to run an idea by her and then I better make a few tuna sandwiches because it's going to be a long night in the library because this is a tough course and I know that I'm going to have to read the chapter twice and it looks like I'm going to miss the pep rally for the football game."

Kids who are able to delay gratification, organize their time, prioritize, seek help, plan ahead, and take responsibility for their process do well. Kids who are able to acknowledge, embrace, and articulate their learning styles do well. Kids who know that they can read 15 pages an hour of a complicated text book and that they can study for three hours before their brain turns to mush and they need a break also do well.

This is not news.

Kids who stop playing "League of Legends" at one in the morning, so they can get the reading done for their nine a. m. class? Kids who smoke pot and forget they have a paper due? Kids who lie to their professors, lie to their parents, and lie to themselves about how much they are studying? Kids who don't know to ask for help to get their stuff done? They do less well.

I met a seemingly well-intentioned father the other day who was ready to write a check for two million dollars to facilitate his child's admission to a "top" school. I could not help but wonder how much he was willing to spend to keep her there.

Here's a not so secret formula: stop spending time, effort, and money on worrying about where your children will go to college. Invest your treasure on focusing on who your children are.

Because no matter where you go, there you are.

Oh, and here's the "secret" of the "success" of the scam artist charging hundreds of thousands of dollars purporting to have cracked the formula for admission to top colleges. This swindle has been around since the 30s but every generation brings newer and more naive sheep. The guy in the trench coat promises to "get your child in" to a top college or your money back. This time the fraud has a "formula;" years ago he "knew someone" in admissions. Either way, the promise of "I'll get your kid in to a top college or your money back" is made to a number of feckless families. Statistically, some of them get in. Princeton, Harvard, and Stanford all admit fewer than one student in ten but SOMEBODY gets in. The huckster tells your kid to play the tuba or to volunteer at the nursing home. Or he gives your kid some magic beans.

In any case, if the student doesn't get admitted to a "top" school, the parents get their money back. If the kid does get admitted the slime-oid laughs all the way to the safety deposit box. It doesn't take too many $200,000 payouts to make a good, if despicable, living.

In the meantime, hard-working, ethical counselors across the country will continue to spread the message: there is no formula that guarantees admission to "top" colleges.

And who your kid is matters more than where she goes.

25

When Will They Ever Learn?

1)   "Turn left at the third light pole before the church that burned down where Lee Ann's grandfather got married that first time."

2)   "Take half the coefficient of the linear term, square it, and add it to both sides."

What do these directives have in common? That not everyone processes information in the same way. Ability and motivation influence learning, but so does background. Where you've been has a lot to do with where you can go. "Say, you're not from around here, are you?" is true in small town America and in ninth grade algebra as well.

Are you feeling lost? Do you not know exactly what to do with finding the family reunion or solving the quadratic? Does driving around small towns in rural Alabama counting light poles--your fancy schmancy GPS doesn't work out HERE, smarty pants!--make you feel nauseated? Are you focusing on that which is not salient to knowing where to turn? I am certainly confused. Because although my high school math if pretty fluent, I am a neophyte when it comes to Southern Directions in this beautiful country with flowing fields and no people to ask where the church used to be. That's why I'm befuddled. I didn't even know Lee Ann's grandfather HAD been married before. I'm focused on whether or not Lee Ann's grandfather's children know. I'm also wondering why the church burned down and whether or not it was insured.

In education, this is what we call "attending to the wrong stimuli."

Whereas in Mathland, I know my way around pretty well. I even know to make sure that the coefficient of the quadratic term in equal to one before doing all that business about squaring and adding.

Let's stop driving around aimlessly and come right to the point about your child who is doing badly in math: What makes you think that your child CAN complete the square? Because YOU are good at math? Because YOU did well in high school algebra?

Or because what you want for your child has overtaken your good sense about what she is capable of producing? Has your uncertainty about the future clouded your good sense to the point where you have mistaken ought for is?

What is the most parsimonious explanation for your daughter's bad grade in math? That she WANTS to do poorly? That she CHOSE not to study? Believe me: if she knew HOW to study, she would study. If there were any evidence to support your belief that the more she studies the more she knows and the better she performs on exams, then she would. What are you arguing? That she WANTS to do badly? Because if your suggestion is that she would do better if only she wanted to, then you might as well say that I WANTED to get lost looking for the third light pole near where the church burned down, that I somehow enjoy being lost, cold, late, and stressed.

Here's my directed advice regarding your child and her poor performance in math: stop yelling at her; stop being disappointed; stop rolling your eyes; stop telling your friends how your daughter would do better in math if only she would try harder, do her homework, care more, stand on her head. To the contrary, remain calm, hire a tutor, consider dropping down a level, restrict access to glowing rectangles, be supportive, focus on motivation rather than results.

I would call you to congratulate you on your new and improved, stress free relationship with your child except, as I mentioned, my cell phone doesn't work out here by the third light pole near where the church burned down where Lee Ann's grandfather got married the first time.

26

Now Sit Right Back and You'll Hear a Tale

When our sons were six, one of my running buddies and I packed up the canoes and the kids and headed out to the barrier islands conveniently located a hundred yards from the mainland out in Biscayne Bay. After tying the boats to the top of the car and loading the coolers--you've been to weddings with less food--we plied our first graders with tales of "Gilligan's Island," our favorite sixties sitcom.

92

After explaining how the professor could build a radio out of sticks and mud but couldn't fix a hole in a boat, we went on to explain how the characters are in a one-to-one correspondence with the seven deadly sins. (The matchup between Gilligan, The Skipper, Mr. and Mrs. Howell, Ginger, Maryann, and the Professor with gluttony, anger, greed, sloth, lust, envy and pride will be left as an exercise for the curious reader. Hint: Mrs. Howell never actually DID anything, did she?)

Our offspring were oddly silent while being exposed to their shared cultural legacy in the car ride across town. Finally one of the boys spoke up: "So they never got off the island?"

"No, son," my buddy explained. "In every episode, Gilligan messed up the rescue somehow. The castaways were never rescued."

The boys went quiet again for a full moment and then said incredulously, "Dad, why didn't they just use their cell phones?"

I treasure this story not only because the children and I found sea urchins in the warm water by the island and we had sour pickles with our sandwiches, but also because it quantifies for me the differences between the generations: our children, natives to the land of technology and immigrants to the outdoors, are the reverse of their parents. I grew up swimming out to the islands off what is now David Kennedy Park in Coconut Grove. I waited until after 11:00 at night to make a long distance phone call. Readers my age will know that the rates went down at that hour; younger readers will see dial phones only in photographs or museums. In 1974, I called a girl at the University of Florida from my apartment in Madison, Wisconsin; I hope to finish repaying the loan I took out for that call sometime next year.

This week I spoke to domestic clients in California, Massachusetts, and New Hampshire as well as international families in Switzerland,

Spain, Columbia, El Salvador and two in Panama. My biggest issue with my student choosing and applying to colleges from Indonesia is the 12-hour time difference. Morning for me is evening for her so we don't match up as well as we might. These calls are effectively free, once the fixed costs of the computer or smart phone are taken into account.

Which brings me to my point about college admissions and parenting for 2015: choice is hard.

A century and a half ago, the brightest kid in your small town went to college out East; a few other kids went to the state university; lots of other kids didn't attend college at all. There was no social stigma. There was certainly less angst. Last month I had clients paralyzed by decisions: admitted to colleges all over the country, some students visited campuses for the second or third time.

I am not suggesting that life was easier 150 years ago. To the contrary, life was hard without antibiotics or anesthesia. Information was hard to come by; no idea could travel faster than the fastest horse. And effective medications were the stuff of science fiction--a genre that had also not yet been invented. Our children now have too much information. As I am not the first to remark, every book ever written, every song ever sung, every idea ever thought is available to every child with an Internet connection. (Read: every child whose parent is considering this essay.) Much of this information--violent pornography, for example--is impossible for children to process.

Gentle guidance? Fewer choices and only developmentally appropriate ones will help your kids grow up strong and centered. "Would you like to wear the red shirt or the blue shirt?" for first graders. "Would you prefer to set the table or take out the trash?" for middle schoolers.

Even "Which movie would you like to watch?" can be a little intimidating and "Which college will you attend?" and "What do

94

you want to do with the rest of your life?" can be downright threatening. In many instances, less is indeed more.

Of course, the best questions of all remain, "Do you want another sour pickle on your sandwich?" and "How many sea urchins have we found?"

27

The Toughest Love of All

You know that guy who is unpleasant with you, has been for years?
You know the one I mean. Maybe he's a colleague at work, maybe a
neighbor. Maybe he's the bully in your algebra class, maybe it's your
wife's sister's husband.

Whoever it is, he's always giving you a hard time, telling you to
change, communicating that you're not okay as you are, that there is

something fundamentally wrong with you as a person. It's not just your clothes or your haircut. It's not just your ethnicity, religion, sexual orientation, or where you're from. This guy just doesn't like you for you. He doesn't like what you do, but at a profound level he doesn't like who you ARE.

You may have thought to yourself: What if you were different? What if you were taller? Shorter? Smarter? Dumber? What if you were left-handed? What if you had red hair? What if you played the trombone? What if you had studied engineering rather than philosophy?

As a functioning adult you are able to ignore this guy, get him out of your head, understand that, truly, it's him not you. You know that you are okay the way you are and that his issues have nothing to do with you. You're happy with the choices you've made, the way things have turned out. You know that this idiot's vision of you is absurd. As a result of his negative attitude you keep your distance. You choose not to see him any more than you have to. You walk your dog down another street. You briefly make small talk at the family reunion then move on to chat with other relatives. You have no interest in changing what you do or who you are for this guy. You have no interest in playing the trombone or being left handed for goodness sake. You're certainly not going to go to graduate school or drop out of graduate school on his suggestion. Under no circumstances are you going to devote hours every day to learning mathematics on his uninformed say so. You don't like math, you never have. Why would you study math just because this guy who doesn't like you to begin with says that you should, that you would get along better if you did?

But what if the guy who doesn't like you, who can't accept you the way you are, who wants to change every aspect of your personality, of what you do, of who you are-what if this guy were your parent?

What if, from the day you were born, the person who was supposed to look after you, to take care of you, to give you unconditional love and support was trying to change you? What if you got the feeling that your parents could not accept you for who you were?

We see rather a lot of this sort of thing in the mental health field, tell you the truth.

"I am a highly successful, academic person; my son doesn't do well in school. We never communicate unless we are arguing about homework and academic performance."

"I am a mathematician, but my daughter refuses to study math; we haven't spoken in years."

"My son married outside my religion; he is dead to me."

Tragedy after tragedy, sadness heaped upon sadness.

Rabbi Kushner taught us "Nobody on their deathbed ever said 'I wish I had spent more time at the office.'" I would add that nobody looking back on those brilliant, magnificent, transitory years of parenting ever said, "I wish we had spent more time arguing about homework."

Here's some gentle, directed advice: this Saturday leave the cell phones at home. Skip soccer practice; ignore the homework; leave the dishes. Forget about Facebook; disregard your email; snub your work responsibilities.

Instead, grab your kid and drive for an hour. Or hop on public transportation. Go to the woods. Take a walk.

You don't have to say anything. Don't talk about the uncertain future or how there aren't any jobs for children who don't take five advanced placement courses in 10th grade. Just take a walk in the woods with your kid. A two-hour walk is good; a five-hour walk is better if you remember to pack some sandwiches and a water bottle. For extra credit you can pick up a rock and throw it at that tree over there. Up to you. Again, the less talking, the better.

Thirty years from now, call me and tell me whether you remember any homework your child ever did (or didn't do.) But I bet you remember the day you put aside your electronics and blew off all your responsibilities and just went for a silent walk in the woods with your kid.

Because you don't want to be that parent who is always negative in the life of your child. You want your kid to know that you love her just the way she is--even if she doesn't get a PhD in math or marry the person you prefer or get that high paying job or keep the house as clean as you would like or raise your grandchildren as you might have done.

You don't want to be the parent who, when the kids are grown and gone, has that emptiness because you didn't take the time with them when it mattered most and loved them unconditionally.

You just don't.

Because after all, what you think is missing in your child is really about what's missing in you.

Or as a dear friend expressed it to me recently, "There's not enough stuff in the world to fill the hole in my mother's heart."

28

Lesson Learned

One of my running buddies found out a few years ago that a distant relative on his wife's side left the couple some $6000. Malcolm wasn't close with his wife's aunt's second husband so he was equally pleased and saddened by the news of his passing.

"He had a good run," Malcolm's wife Janet agreed. "Ninety-four years old and never sick a day in his life. Died in his own bed and in his own home. Doesn't get much better than that."

"And darn nice of him to leave all nine of you nieces and nephews that money."

Of course, no story in this book is either that simple or straightforward. Because seven of the nine beneficiaries instigated litigation that started ugly and, after three and a half years, got uglier. Apparently everyone getting together for a nice meal to share remembrances, talk old times, and celebrate the life of the deceased was not in the cards.

It seems that Janet's uncle had been taken care of by one of her mom's cousins who was disappointed that his share wasn't bigger than those of the other children who hadn't been active participants in their uncle's last years. Of course the other children disagreed. Attorneys were hired; words were spoken; relationships were broken irretrievably.

Oh, and the amount in dispute? Were one set of cousins to win, their six thousand dollar share would have increased to around seven thousand dollars. The "losing" cousins would have seen their six thousand dollar share go down to some $5K.

My buddy was philosophical about the carnage, but I had to ask. Why would your wife's relatives fight so hard about such a small differential of money? Are these folks the poster children for "too much time on their hands?" Were they mad at each other from some previous incident? Were they arithmetically impaired--unable to guess that the attorneys would earn more than anyone else?

Malcolm was introspective. "I don't think so," he said. "When I asked the cousins why they were fighting so hard with one another they said that they wanted to teach each other a lesson and to make sure the same thing didn't happen again."

"To teach each other a lesson so that the same thing didn't happen again?"

"Yeah I guess if their uncle were to die again. Of course, he would have to come back to life or something first."

***

Why is this family destroying itself over a trivial amount of money that means nothing to any of them? Why are they willing to never speak to one another again for the rest of their lives for a thousand dollars?

Beats the heck out of me. I don't pretend to have the first insight into human nature. I haven't a clue what these folks were thinking, why they would lose relationships that had gone on for generations over a lousy thousand bucks.

I am supposed to be something of an expert on parenting though. (For a dissenting opinion on my status as expert, feel free to contact any of my four children.) So I will make an analogy to your relationship with your kids: are you fighting hard over that which ultimately makes no significant difference?

Is there such a thing as "leave well enough alone"? If your kid has a 92 average, it is worth all that emotional dissonance to insist that she have a 94? Could an argument be made for "peace in the home"? Could you maybe lessen your anxiety about her grades long enough to go for a bike ride with her to the ice cream place in your neighborhood?

What about taking out the trash? Don't get me wrong. I am all about able-bodied children helping with household chores in general and trash in particular. But there comes a point where a loving parent has to ask the question, "Why are we going to war over a task that takes, on average, just under two minutes?"

Ultimately of course, the kids should be responsible for taking out the trash, no question. But if getting the garbage bucket to the curb involves rending of garments and loss of life, you might want to ask yourself what else might be going on with the family.

Because the answers I typically hear, "If I don't force him to take out the trash now, how will he learn to take out the trash later?" make as much sense as Malcolm's wife's uncle coming back to life.

29

They Are Who They Are

It is coming increasingly clear that "we are who we are." I didn't choose to be a happily married heterosexual male any more than any of my gay friends and relatives chose to be who they are. "Straight Camp"-okay, there's no such thing as "Straight Camp"-doesn't work. How do I know? Why am I so thoroughly convinced that nobody "chooses" to be gay any more than I "choose" not to be? Because you could threaten, coerce, cajole, punish, reward, berate, or beat me. And I would still like women.

You know what I mean. It's just that simple. I like women; I have always liked women; it seems likely that I always will like women—my wonderful wife in particular.

If the smart money is on "we are who we are" when it comes to an issue as fundamental as sexual orientation, why are parents so completely unaccepting when it comes to the abilities of their kids?

Motivation and "time served" have to be the accepted standards. Results are an absurd criteria. Offensive really. Yelling at your kid to like math is like yelling at me not to be attracted to my wife.

Good luck with that.

Yes, we can all try harder; yes, we can all get (marginally) better. Sure, if you went to the gym five days a week instead of two, you would be more likely to get rid of that tire around your tummy. You could stop telling that old joke about keeping your six-pack abs safe behind a protective layer of fat.

Similarly, if you quit your job and devoted yourself full time to running, you could get faster and run longer. But you could still never finish a marathon in less than three hours. You could certainly never compete with Lelisa Desisa of Ethiopia who beat the best in the world at Boston last year. He ran 26.2 miles in two hours nine minutes and something. You could take a taxicab to the 25-mile mark and jump into the race like Rosie Ruiz and he would still beat you by several hundred yards.

And yes, if you studied math day and night, you could improve. But there is a limit to how much better you could get. You know the Reimann Hypothesis that the best mathematical minds on the planet have been assiduously working on since 1859? You're not going to crack it. Given your current knowledge, it would take you a number of years of consistent study just to understand the question.

So why is there this ridiculous discord in your house about the results of your daughter's math class? The only thing worse than yelling at your daughter about her math grade is yelling at your daughter about her *rank* in class. "As long as she's in the top ten percent, I'll be happy."

This just in: not everyone can be in the top ten percent. Think about it: By definition, only ten percent of the children can be in the top ten percent.

Encouraging your daughter to see her classmates as obstacles to be overcome rather than colleagues to help along leads us to Deborah Meier's wonderful example of the kindergarten teacher telling the children to line up to go out to recess. Deborah tells the story better, but it goes something like this: "Okay, children, we are going to line up for recess. I want each one of you to be first in line. No pushing, no shoving."

I love this story because it makes perfect sense at first glance as I think of one adorable five-year-old making her way to the front of the line. But when I think of *all* those precious kindergarten kids scrambling to be first, I realize how absurd it is to have them compete.

The ideas in this essay can be summarized as follows:

Not everyone can be first. It is demeaning to your child to make her success contingent upon the failure of her classmates.

If you must praise your child for her accomplishments-rather than just loving her unconditionally-focus on her motivation and effort rather than on her results.

106

Accept your kid for who she is-even if she never wins the Boston Marathon or gets an A in calculus.

And whatever you do, don't try to change who your kid is regarding which partners they find attractive-because they are who they are.

30

Choice Parenting

1) Four-year-old Liam picks a wooden train out of the toy box. His six-year-old brother, Colby, comes over and grabs the train from his hand. Undeterred, Liam gathers a bag of blocks and starts to build a tower. Colby knocks over the stack of blocks. Undaunted, Liam selects a puzzle. Before he has put together the first two pieces, Colby pushes Liam out of the way and starts to work on the puzzle.

Having had quite enough of his older brother, Liam takes the box of pattern blocks, goes into his room, and locks the door to play by himself. Colby stands outside the closed door and inquires, "What's the matter? Don't you want to play anymore?"

2) A twenty-something graduate student calls her mother's mother. Before the young woman can say, "Hi, grandma, how are you?" she hears, "It's about time you called; I haven't heard from you in weeks. I was so worried. Are you okay? Why don't I hear from you more often?"

When the grandmother hangs up after a brief conversation, she ponders out loud, "I wonder why she doesn't call more often."

These situations which are so blindingly obvious to us with the viewpoint of our seats in the balcony are not at all clear to the participants caught up in the action in real time: Colby is having a perfectly good day, bullying his little brother, taking all his toys. Six-year-olds are not known for "perspective taking", seeing the point of view of another person. Colby doubtless believes that he and Liam are indeed "playing." Colby's needs are being met. He gets whichever toy he wants; he gets to push his little brother around.

Perhaps the grandmother in the situation is getting her needs met as well: she is expressing her anxiety, communicating that the world is an uncertain place, making it known that she wishes her grandchild would call more often. Perhaps she is angry about being widowed after a 53-year marriage and strikes out where ever she can.

It's hard to know exactly why another person behaves as she does.

What is clear is that Liam is going to think long and hard about sharing or playing with his sibling subsequently. The 20-something graduate student is going to reflect on whether or not she wants to reach out to her grandmother next time she has a minute between classes, papers, and exams.

Before we dismiss the examples above with an emphatic, "Well, duh! Of course, Colby should be more gracious. Obviously, the grandmother should bottle her negativity" let's ask ourselves these questions: Are there blind spots in our own lives that are as glaringly apparent as the ones in the examples above? When we look back at our interactions with our kids, will we feel like we have done everything that we could have to have healthy relationships? Or will we come to understand that we would have handled some situations differently were we given the chance to go through those precious years again. (Note: we will NOT be given the chance to bring up our children differently. In the game of life, there are no Mulligans.)

How is it possible that there is constant conflict and strife in our relationships with our--in my dad's favorite phrase--"beloved children"?

Could it be that our needs were not met by our own parents and that we are looking for care from the next generation?

If our own parents didn't nurture us, care for us, listen to us, let us grow, meet our needs, are we hoping that our own children can fill those gaps?

If we are looking for help from our kids rather than from our parents, we are going to the wrong place. Our job as parents is to provide emotional support and stability for our kids. It is our responsibility to take care of them. It is not their job to take care of us.

Here's an admittedly silly, but provoking question: would you rather have a child who was successful and fulfilled but got in touch infrequently or a child who was a "hot mess" but kept in constant touch? Would you be happy with a daughter who was a happily married orthopedic surgeon and a mother of three who was too busy to spend much time with you? Or would you prefer a kid living in

110

your basement at age 30 who emerged frequently to ask how you were doing-then borrowed your credit card again to sign up for another month of "Shoot, Shoot, Shoot, Kill, Kill, Kill, Blood, Blood, Blood"?

For the purposes of this hypothetical, a child who is both content and communicative is not an option.

Which would you choose? The happy child who doesn't keep in touch or the miserable child who does? Couldn't it be argued that one sign of good mental health in our children is their ability to live independently?

Wouldn't you agree that a child who calls you because he wants to is preferable to a child who gets in touch because of guilt?

The good news is that in real life, a child who is both content and successful as well as attentive and thoughtful is a real possibility.

There was a 60s bumper sticker that read, "If you love something, let it go; if it comes back, it's yours. If it doesn't, it never was."

Although your children are a gift, they are not yours to control nor do they belong to you. Their respect for their parents must be earned; their affection can never be commanded.

31

Parenting Without Grades

Remember the best teacher you had in high school, the one from whom you learned so much? Ever reflect on why she never had any discipline problems? Was it because your classmates were more respectful in those halcyon years? That teacher seemed so relaxed, in control, no behavior management issues. Were the students more attentive because she was more interesting, because she knew more material, because she was more strict? Or was it her relaxed attitude that allowed everyone to learn? Was she, in actuality, LESS strict?

Was she relaxed because her students were attentive or were the students attentive because she was relaxed?

Imagine a parent who is constantly going on line to the school website to check her son's grades. "Why do you have a missing homework in math?" she intones. "I turned those assignments in," her son replies. "The teacher just hasn't entered the grades yet."

As you might envisage, this conversation rapidly descends down a rabbit hole from which there is no return as accusations and prevarications escalate in an explosive spiral. "That's what you said last time!" mom shouts. "Why don't you trust me?" her son replies.

Consider to the contrary a parent who never discusses his son's grades, never goes on line to check. Is the mother checking up on the first student BECAUSE he's doing poorly? Or is the student not doing well in school BECAUSE his mother is constantly crossing a boundary and impinging on his autonomy?

If I thought that by constant checking your son's grades and obsessing over every assignment that you could turn a sow's ear into a silk purse-ignoring that you would still have an unhappy pig-I would be willing to consider the option and suggest that you enroll in the Sherlock Holmes School of Parenting. But I have never, in 40 years of teaching met a child whose grades improved as a result of hyper-vigilance on the part of the parents. And consider the hidden agenda; what is being communicated "between the lines":

1)   I don't trust you to care about your grades on your own.

2)   I care more about your grades than I do about our relationship.

3)   You are fundamentally not okay as a person unless your grades are good.

4)   I have way too much time on my hands.

The father who doesn't check his son's grades communicates that he likes his kid for who he is, not for what the kid achieves. Should it turn out that his son would be more content working as a carpenter's assistant rather than getting a Ph.D. in philosophy, dad is okay with that. Dad has his own life to live; he cannot be bothered going to high school a second time.

Even more importantly, by not going on line to check grades, dad saves his high trump cards for if and when he needs them. He is able to help his son distinguish that which is critical-don't take drugs-from that which is much less important-get good grades.

Lastly, the dad who trusts his kid to find his own path allows his child to individuate. "I would give you a kidney if you needed it" dad communicates, "but I acknowledge that we are distinct being and that I cannot live your life for you."

As parents, I'm not sure it gets any better than that.

32

How Can You Have Any Pudding...

That Miami, my cherished hometown, has only two seasons is well known. "Construction and hurricane" rather than the traditional four enumerated in the James Taylor song is what we have in South Florida and I'm used to it after almost 60 examples of each. What the tourist brochures neglect to mention is that with the advent of summer come swarms of mosquitoes in numbers that can only be described as Biblical. Having recently spent a few minutes swatting, slapping, scratching, fidgeting, cursing, lighting citronella candles, spraying carcinogens all over my body and--don't try this at home-- putting on thick wool socks to dissuade the ravenous beasties, I was still covered in bug bites the size of Brazil. Discretion being the better part of valor, I finally listened to my imminently sensible wife who suggested that I consider coming inside the house.

What a concept. All that slapping, whacking, and scratching to no discernible purpose when all I needed to do was walk a few steps to casa firma.

Trying to extinguish the multitude of behaviors we don't like in our children is similar to trying to smack each and every one of the hoards of blood sucking creepy-crawlies in South Florida. Yes, the whining and demanding of children at many ages could cause a loving parent to want to put her foot through a stained glass window[1]. But if your life resembles an unrelenting series of "put that down," "don't do that," and "how many times do I have to tell you?" then maybe it's time to take a step back. I'm not suggesting that your advice to your children is incorrect--I am the first to agree that a cat does not belong on a ceiling fan--only that you might want to consider the age old parenting adage: "pick 'em." Because some of what you're fighting for is likely not worth dying over.

I invite you to consider some of the bad advice you received from adults when you were a kid. Think of the BAD advice, the thoroughly discredited advice, the unequivocally disproven advice, the blatantly S-T-O-O-P-I-D advice with which you grew up and which you miraculously managed to get beyond (for the most part anyway.) After painstaking research including thinking about picking up the phone and actually calling another human being for help, I was able to come up with the following egregious example:

---

[1] This metaphor is an homage to Raymond Chandler who used it to greater advantage when describing the effect of an attractive woman on a Bishop

We had a family friend growing up who insisted that we finish all the food on our plates before we could drink any fluids. This mom's "thinking," such as it was, involved a convoluted tribute to "children starving in Europe" and an 18th century conceptualization of human digestion. The thought that elementary aged children could determine on their own whether or not they were thirsty would have been denounced in favor of an assertion that "children should be seen and not fed."

In all seriousness, even as a child, I detected an agenda of power and control.

I'm going to go out on a limb here and suggest that if your child's emotional needs are being met, it is less likely that he will devote his life to making yours miserable. If you and your son are going for a walk with the dog, talking about nothing, and throwing rocks at that tree over there in the empty lot, there is less chance that said child will have enough time to find a way to put the words "duct tape," "cat," and "ceiling fan" in the same sentence.

How does a life become an unending series of "load the dishwasher," "do your homework," and "why don't I ever hear from you?" Don't get me wrong. I am in favor of all these behaviors: I voted for the "take out the trash" candidate in 2014; I supported the "A in algebra" platform in 2016, and will donate money to the "my child should call me more frequently" nominee in 2018.

I just wonder how it all got so crazy. I have to believe that in a loving family where "everybody works, everybody eats" and where we all enjoy just being with one another and where we value each other even if some of us don't have an A in algebra, there might exist children who WANT to help out because they actually CARE about the larger people who live down the hall.

Especially if those said larger people are perceived as being on the same team, a team that enjoys hanging out together, taking walks, and talking about nothing. If the people on that team have read Winnie the Pooh and The Forgotten Door together rather than forcing one another to eat eggs over easy before allowing them to have a sip of milk, there might be fewer duct taped felines spinning overhead.

33

The Language of Heroism

Harry Zuckerman was a big part of my life growing up. He drove car pool to Sunday school and had been my dad's best friend in law school. Harry married LaVona in late December 1954, two weeks after my mom and dad got hitched. "For tax purposes," both couples explained. The joke was that by getting married late in the year they could claim deductions on their 1040s. Even as a child I knew that both couples were, in my dad's phrase, "deeply and madly" in love.

Harry never talked about his experiences overseas. "Everyone has World War Two stories," he said. Actually, I wasn't so sure. Certainly, some number of people had parachuted into occupied France with the 82nd Airborne, but not everyone surely. Harry's modesty and protestations to the contrary notwithstanding, it still sounded like extraordinary heroism.

I got stories about Harry from my dad: Harry boxing Bantam-weight in Brooklyn (did they even wear *gloves* in those days?); Harry eking out an uncertain living from 70-hour weeks with a push cart during the depression; Harry running six miles in 36 minutes. In full combat gear. And then that bit about jumping out of a perfectly good airplane through a hail of bullets into a country crawling with people who were more than willing to kill you with a bayonet.

A few months before he enlisted, Harry determined that it would be to his advantage to speak German. So he learned German. He already knew Yiddish so maybe German wasn't that much of a stretch. He also learned French. Next time you're arguing with your child trying to convince him to memorize ten Spanish vocabulary words for the quiz tomorrow, think about a man learning two languages fluently in a matter of months on the off chance that he would need them when he got shipped overseas.

Through some unrecorded acts of heroism on the part of some boys who didn't come home, Harry got a "battlefield promotion." That is to say, all the officers above him in rank were killed, so he became a lieutenant. In charge of hundreds of prisoners of war, Harry's facility in German came in handy just as he has predicted. "Put your weapons over there" he ordered.

"Ah, I can tell from you accent that you are from Dusseldorf" said the commanding officer of the captured forces. Harry felt no obligation to point out that Dusseldorf was some distance--both geographically and metaphorically--from a pushcart in Brooklyn.

120

Just as everyone had a WWII story when I was growing up, today everyone has a story like the following: Lucius refuses to have dinner with the family. He eats in his room by himself while playing video games and he won't eat anything unless we get him pizza with pepperoni and pineapple from that Italian place across town. We got him a limo for his prom but he isn't the least bit appreciative and we believe that his pot and alcohol use are increasing.

This narrative may be even farther from both Depression-era Brooklyn and occupied France.

I am not arguing that there are any salutary effects to watching your buddies be slaughtered by machine gun fire. I am hardly recommending that your children need to starve in order to appreciate healthy food. I am pointing out that no child ever in the history of the world was born with the money, the moral authority, or the innate desire to buy a PlayStation, to insist on certain menus, to be thoroughly disconnected from his family. If a child in your home is having his brain sucked dry hour after hour by violent video games rather than learning something from reading a book, hanging out with his parents, learning a language, or interacting with other members of his species, it is because YOU brought the enormous electronic turd into your house and allowed these borderline anti-social behaviors. Your kid doesn't have any money, for goodness sake; he's a kid. You bought the thing. You allow the outrage. Of course he's going to become addicted to violent video games if you allow him to. You might as well just buy him heroin and teach him how to use the needle.

But I digress.

Why are you allowing your child to eat pineapple and pepperoni pizza in his room rather than engaging in conversation and shared chores with his family? Where did these behaviors come from?

121

Too much leniency when the children were younger? Too much control? Were your expectations too high, not high enough? Could you have loved your children unconditionally? Should you have taken a day off from work to take your kids on a hike? Are you too invested in having your kid like you? Are you trying to achieve "peace in our time" in your home? Are you scared of a little conflict?

Speaking of WWII, those of you who know the least little bit about Chamberlain's visit to Hitler in 1939 will appreciate the irony of the phrase "peace in our time". As to WHY you feel that it is critical that your children like you to the point that you capitulate and buy them violent video games, I would not presume to say.

I would suggest that a sense of shared purpose is what helps to shape heroes. If jumping out of an airplane into occupied France isn't on the syllabus, at least joining the family for a meal should be.

Parents have more influence on their children than they can possibly imagine. Using that influence for good is your sacred duty. You can lay the groundwork for bringing up a hero as easily as you can pave the way for an isolating addict.

Let's all agree to take our best shot.

34

Wild Life

Feeling fairly confident that the children were old enough to take a walk in Myakka River State Park by themselves, but not confident enough to actually let them leave the campsite unattended in the dark, I accompanied them down the trail into the woods. Before we had walked a hundred steps, the kids saw a pair of glowing yellow eyes 20 feet up in a tree. To this day, my kids and the assorted school friends who came camping with us, are convinced that we spotted one of the few remaining Florida Panthers.

After staring at the incandescent orbs for several awestruck seconds, the children determined that their evolutionary adaptive environment had left them ill prepared to cope with a Puma concolor in the wild, that their nine-year-old fingernails and teeth would not fare well "mano a paw-o" with a 130 pound carnivore who makes its living killing and eating small mammals were the creature to determine that my kids were indeed small and mammalian. In short, they were scared. So we returned to the campsite to pick up one large stick of firewood each. Thus armed, we returned to our hike where--and I am totally fine with this--nothing else noteworthy happened whatsoever.

A decade and a half later, my kids and I still occasionally refer to "the camping trip when we maybe saw a panther in a tree." I imagine that the statistics and science courses the children took in college have allowed them to come to understand that the animal in the tree was more than likely "only" a raccoon, common as dirt in our region. The chance that one of the hundred and something remaining Florida panthers was "hanging around" (sorry) in a tree a hundred yards from a campsite replete with giggling fifth graders was equivalent to the chance that a man my age could sleep through the night in a tent without needing to find his flip flops and stumble to the bathroom. But I am still overwhelmed with the poignancy and magic of the moment.

The next day, after a healthful breakfast of sugary cereal eaten straight out of the box, the kids asked me questions about evolutionary biology, Florida history, the development of the State Park System, and why we had once again forgotten to bring enough marshmallows. Obviously, I didn't know the answers to any of the questions but it was glorious to watch the developing intellect of the kids and to start feeling sorry for any middle school teachers they might encounter the following year.

124

Contrast the story of "the camping trip when we maybe saw a panther in a tree" with the narrative of "the trip where we stood in line for 45 minutes in the sun before going on that ride where Jamie threw up and then pitched a boogie because her second ice cream cone melted and we refused to buy her a twelve-dollar lollipop." And don't even get me started on "the trip to the mall where they didn't have anything in my size." Where are the memories more likely to come from? I take the campfire over the amusement park or the mall any day.

You know why nobody likes telemarketers? It's not just that they try to sell you crap you don't need, but because by definition, they don't know who you are or what you might want. You reflexively hang up on them because they don't know you. Why would you listen to someone let alone purchase something from someone who doesn't have any ideas what your needs are or what is important to you?

You wouldn't and you don't.

You listen to the sermons at your house of worship because you have chosen to attend. You listen to the political views of your dinner companions because you invited them to share a meal. You don't listen to random strangers calling you at dinnertime.

I met with a successful woman recently and her 11 year-old son. "Diego" was doing poorly in school in spite of his gifted IQ and the fact that he was reading three years ahead of grade level. His testing confirmed that he had no learning differences or attentional issues.

Maybe I was imagining things, but when mom was haranguing her son about his motivation, study skills, classroom performance and lousy report cards, I got the distinct impression that Diego thought he was listening to a telemarketer. The doors behind his eyes slammed shut like the gates at a secure facility. I felt like I was watching two strangers talking about a volatile political topic about which they vehemently disagreed. They certainly weren't listening to one another.

Forty years ago when I first started counseling children and their families about how to improve their results at school, I might have talked to this family about a behavioral contract and some academic tutoring. Twenty years ago, I might have advocated taking away the video games until Diego paid more attention to his homework. Last week listening to these sad, angry people, I gave them the only advice that I think might make a long term, significant difference.

I asked mom if she could take a weekend off from work, shut down her cell phone and not return any emails for two solid days. When she said she might be able to, I handed her a dirty map, sticky with bits of stale marshmallows.

Of Myakka River State Park.

I hope this nice woman is able to sleep through the night without having to get up and stumble to the bathroom in the dark. And I most fervently wish that she and Diego will take a walk after dinner. Because who knows? Maybe Diego and his mom will see a pair of glowing eyes 20 feet up in a tree.

That experience will give this family something excruciatingly wonderful to talk about years down the road.

Assuming of course those fiery eye balls DON'T actually belong to one of the few remaining Florida panthers and that the panther isn't in the mood for chomping on a small mammal.

35

The No-Tell Motel

My wife says I could have an extramarital affair.

But that I would have to go north of Orlando.

Because there is no out of the way restaurant, no hotel, no aisle in Publix, no hospital waiting room where I don't run into friends or old students or someone whom I know from my 59 years in Miami.

I was graduated from Coral Gables High in 1973. And in spite of some defections to northern climes, there are a number of my classmates still bumping around here in South Florida. To discourage any hope of a clandestine assignation, there are also family friends everywhere in this burg. My dad was graduated from UM law in 1953. I see his classmates and their children and grandchildren in the gym and on the street. My mom was "Edison High, class of '41." (Go Red Raiders!) before she taught at the University of Miami. To this day when my mom and I are out together we will bump into her old students who shyly ask, "Are you Miss Cohen?" "Well, I was," my mom will reply pointing to me. "Before I met his father and got married in 1954."

I wasn't particularly thinking of stepping out on my wife when the two of us were visiting colleges and rehab programs in obscure New Hampshire towns recently. (Only the snarkiest of my gentle readers would have the lack of breeding to point out that many towns in New Hampshire might qualify as obscure.) But sure enough, as Patti and I were crossing a street, there turning into a driveway was a close friend from Miami. "Good to see you, David" she called, as if she had every expectation of bumping into me a thousand miles from the school both our daughters attend. "Good to see you too, Joanne," I replied.

My wife--not a woman who is frequently at a loss for words--was dumbfounded. "Canada," she muttered.

"Canada?" I asked.

"Canada," she repeated. "If you wanted to have an extra-marital affair, you'd have to go to Canada."

Not one to miss an opportunity no matter how abstract, I inquired, "Don't you think you'd know if I were gone for days at a time?"

128

My wife, now back on her game, acknowledged that she would indeed notice my absence and infidelity before chopping me up into little pieces and feeding me to the family dog.

Whether or not we no longer live in communities where "everybody knows everybody" is an open question. I would point out that there do seem to be some values in a place. Not values in the sense of "something good" but values meaning "shared understandings."

In public and private schools in Miami, for example, everyone knows a kid from whom he can buy prescription painkillers. A shared understanding among kids is that drugs are ubiquitous at their schools. Indeed, I defy you to find a middle school child who will not respond to the query, "Do you know someone in your class from whom you could buy psycho-stimulants?" in the affirmative. Admittedly, you might have to change "psycho-stimulants" in the above sentence to "ADD pills" but you get the idea. Indeed for years, I have been asking kids in my office "How long would it take you to buy marijuana at your school?" The most common response is, "maybe 20 minutes."

The outlier I heard recently was from an 11th grader from a small town in Utah. He asked me to clarify what I meant by "drugs." When I said, "marijuana, I guess," he replied, "Twenty minutes." "What about cocaine then?" I continued. "Oh, that would take longer," he said. "I would have to go over to the next town." And then not wanting to disappoint me I suppose, he continued. "But I could be back in just over an hour."

So if nowhere in the country is safe-no small town or big city, no school public or private-how do we keep our kids from drugs?

I will give my thoughtful readers some time to respond with their insights before adding my thoughts in subsequent books.

In the meantime, I will continue not to give any thought to isolated Northeastern towns in which I could have an unreported assignation.

36

May I Give You Some Advice?

One of my running buddies has a neighbor who gives her endlessly sincere advice about her workouts. He has insights into her weekly mileage, speed work, the long run, recovery, cross training, you name it. Her neighbor pontificates about the newest training schedule he has heard about. Jennifer is a gifted athlete who has qualified and run the Boston marathon several times. She has logged enough training miles to have run around the world at the equator. She listens patiently.

To her neighbor who could not run from his kitchen to his bedroom.

When he finally stops talking, she goes out for her run.

Robert has a neuro-typical child who was graduated at the top of her high school class before heading off to a top college and law school. Daniel's son is on the autism spectrum, has moderate speech delays, and is unresponsive to many communications from his loving parents. Daniel's son's behavior at home and at school in ungovernable and includes yelling, throwing things, and rolling on the floor. Yet Robert incessantly gives Daniel advice as if the two children weren't 20 years apart in age and a thousand miles apart in makeup.

"I never allowed my child to act that way," Robert begins. "It is NOT okay for a second grader to hit his mom. When my daughter was that age, she was already reading on a high school level..."

Robert's advice is neither helpful not wanted. To the contrary, I have often wondered why Daniel doesn't just come out and say, "We've already thought of that; we already know that; we've already tried that." No one would blame Daniel if he went on to say, "Children are different. Are you trying to be helpful or just bragging again about how your daughter got a scholarship to law school?" before suggesting that Robert take a long walk off a short pier.

Maybe Daniel could be snarky enough to suggest that Robert spend a day with Daniel's developmentally delayed and unmanageable son. I suspect that Robert would be uncomfortable trying to walk a mile in those moccasins, that he would think twice about giving advice having tried to get Daniel's son to put on his shoes let alone finish his homework.

132

Which brings me to the ultimate in ironic advice: you may wish to stop giving so much advice to your children.

I'm not suggesting that your children are on the spectrum and that you cannot understand their behavior because of your neuro-typical brain. I am suggesting that your children are intimately well acquainted with your suggestions.

Of course I could be completely wrong: Maybe what your children need is to be told for the one hundred and first time that you expect them to do well in pre-calculus.

But my guess is that they already know your opinion. Taking a step back and trying to take the perspective might be helpful. Why might your daughter's eyes glaze over when you tell her--again--about how you did well in school? Why might your son suddenly remember an appointment when you tell him about how he should run faster?

Last point: the irony of my giving you advice about why you should consider giving your children less advice is not lost on me. Do you think I should ask Jennifer's neighbor what he thinks I should do?

37

First Step

Alex's defiance has been escalating since middle school and is no longer passive. In eighth grade he said, "I'll take out the garbage as soon as I go up one more level." At 17, he says, "I hate this house and everyone in it; on my next birthday, I never have to see either of you two losers ever again."

Mom suggests that without a high school diploma or marketable skills of any kind, Alex will have a tough time coming up with first and last month's rent. Dad asks about Alex's marijuana usage. Alex indignantly swears that he has smoked pot "only three times." Dad feels strongly that "only three times" refers not to lifetime consumption but rather to "this morning."

School is an unrelenting nightmare for the family. Electronic communication proceeds formal letter leading to conference after conference: Alex is disengaged; Alex is skipping class; Alex isn't turning in assignments; Alex is disrespectful to teachers.

Alex's conduct at home is even worse: his behavior is unmanageable. He refuses to do any household chores whatsoever; when he doesn't get his way regarding curfew, he becomes belligerent. Although he has never actually hit either parent, the threat of physical violence is never far from the surface. Recently, when his mother tried to wake him up to go to school, Alex pushed her and hurt her shoulder.

Alex's parents are at a loss. Alex's psychologist suggests that Alex will mature over time. Alex's parents aren't sure they have much time given Alex's predilection for drinking and driving. Alex's psychiatrist recommends adding an atypical antipsychotic medication to Alex's regiment of psycho-stimulants for attention and SSRIs for anxiety. Alex's parents don't think the current medicines are making any difference and can't get any clarity on the interaction between the prescription meds that they know Alex is taking and the street drugs that they don't.

Just when Alex's parents don't feel the situation can get any worse, Alex is arrested for burglary and possession. "We were just hanging out in the backyard by the pool," Alex explains. "And the drugs weren't even mine. How many times do I have to tell you?"

Whether or not the parents believe Alex's series of half-truths and blatant prevarications becomes less important than the judge's opinion. It is becoming increasingly likely that Alex will have to spend time in jail.

Alex's educational consultant working with his defense attorney suggests that Alex enroll in a wilderness behavioral program rather than go to prison.

The only problem, according to Alex's parents, is that he won't go to wilderness therapy voluntarily.
"Many children refuse the idea at first," says the educational consultant. "There are escort services that accompany recalcitrant youth to the outdoor program."

"You mean big guys who show up in the early hours of the morning?" asks Alex's father.

"That would never work," agrees Alex's mother. "Alex would fight them."

"He would punch and kick," Alex's father goes on. "He played lacrosse in middle school and he still has the stick near his bed."

"If they wake him up at 4:00 in the morning, he will put his foot through the bathroom window and run away.

Without another viable option, Alex's parents fill in the paperwork for a wilderness therapy program out west and agree to have Alex picked up by professional transporters.

"But be careful," Alex's mom cautions the team. "He will probably be stoned and asleep, but he can be violent."

"And he's very strong especially when he's angry," seconds Alex's dad.

136

At 4:00 am the next morning, Alex's parents nervously admit the transport team into their home then walk down the block so that they don't have to hear the ensuing outburst and violence. Surprisingly, they hear no noise of any kind and, moments later, see their son walking calmly to the car.

In their conversation with the transporters later that day, the parents ask what happened.

"Alex is safely at the program," the transporter says.

"But wasn't he aggressive? Didn't he curse at you and try to punch you?" Alex's mom asks.

"No," the transporter responds. "To the contrary, he was polite and thoughtful. Everything went smoothly."

"But what did he say?" asks Alex's dad. "When you picked him up and explained where you were going, what did he say?"

"He said, 'Where have you been? What took you so long? I've been waiting for years, hoping you'd show up.'"

***

Sometimes that which we fear the most for our kids is exactly what they need the most. Sometimes the behaviors that seem most ingrained are just the ones that the kids want to get rid of as well. Sometimes the only way to overcome a fear of cold water is to jump into cold water.

Alex's parents were concerned about Alex's pot use, school failure, aggression, and oppositionality.

As it happens, Alex was concerned as well. He just didn't know how to ask for help or start living a different life.

The more your children seem happy living contrary to their parents' wishes, the more likely it is that the kids want to experience the power of transformative positive change just as much as their parents do.

Oh, and what happened to Alex? How is he doing down the road? Alex went on to a therapeutic boarding school after wilderness therapy. It has now been a full ten years since he was arrested for burglary and first met with his educational consultant.

His mom called me a few months ago. To tell me that Alex had finished his Master's in Business and was working for the C.O.O. of a Fortune 400 firm. He has been clean and sober for a decade and volunteers one evening a week working with young addicts in recovery.

A journey of a thousand miles begins with a single step. Indeed, that first step can be harder than all the rest of the steps put together.

38

Winning Argument

How do my readers who are FOX News aficionados feel about devotees of MSNBC? And those of you who love the Daily Show with John Stewart, what are your thoughts about folks who never miss an installment of Rush Limbaugh?

Do you view the purveyors of contrary opinions with dislike bordering on antipathy? Do you feel a visceral aversion akin to antagonism? Don't you just want to strangle those blockheads on the other channel? How can they just not get it? It's so obvious! The correct opinion is as plain as the nose on my face!

Would it surprise you to learn that you have more in common with these folks with whom you "have nothing in common" than it might appear? Yes, you disagree on every Supreme Court decision; yes, you disagree on every headline from gay marriage to immigration and from gun control to abortion.

But what you may have in common is the **intensity** of your beliefs and the emotionality behind your views.

Think about it for a moment: is there any chance, any measurable probability, that your side is going to win? The Dolphins may beat the Patriots in the AFC championship game this year, but the Fins are not going to beat New England in every game going forward for seasons untold. Do you think that the Protestants can emerge victorious over the Catholics in Northern Ireland? Do you think that any of the warring factions in the Middle East can defeat their opponents once and for all?

The endgame is not winning one game of chess and putting the pieces away. The last position on the board is Rwanda in 1996.

Or as Orwell pointed out writing a few years after the end of WWII, the *object* of the "two-minute hate" is immaterial. As long as the populace is manipulated into investing in mindless angry bellowing, the country at which the invective is directed doesn't much matter.

Especially to our children.

As always, kids learn what they live. And it matters little what their parents are yelling about. A vegetarian mom screaming about the evils of consuming dead animals and a meat eating dad shouting about "those stupid vegetarians" convey the same information--that

140

the world is not a secure place and that there are people who are so wrong that they merit being screamed about.

Don't misunderstand: I'm in favor of some of the topics mentioned above and against others just like you. I vote, engage in discourse, read opinions, and sometimes even watch television. It's just that I invariably see the exact same show across channels, commentators, and beliefs. I watch well-researched, brilliant insights conveyed with impeccable timing, but I also am overwhelmed by the outrage and heartlessness. Disgrace! Scandal! Can you even believe what those idiots did next? How could anyone do such a thing?

Children benefit from calm; the medium is indeed the message.

You might even want to be quiet long enough to allow your kids to get a word in edgewise. So that they grow up knowing that their opinions are valued. No one was ever persuaded of anything by an argument that began with the words, "Jane, you ignorant slut."

Next time you want to express sputtering indignation at the barbarity of the other side, the sheer stupidity of their beliefs, take a step back and a deep breath. Children need to know that their parents are in control. Children also need to understand that they are respected and loved--even if they do turn out to be Protestants or Catholics, gay or straight, Democrats or Republicans, Sunnis or Shiites.

The alternative--out of control outrage and frequent sputtering-- makes kids feel unsafe. And like their only alternative is to internalize, and then act out on, their unremitting hostility.

39

A Deal Is A Deal

Of all the brilliant Dave Barry lines, "You can't make this stuff up" remains high on my list--an extension of Mark Twain's, "Truth is stranger than fiction because fiction has to make sense."

A Florida couple was recently arrested for giving marijuana and cocaine to their middle school children in order to encourage the kids to go to school, do their homework, that sort of thing.

142

Yes, I wish I were making this up.

But there is a lesson here for all loving parents and no, that lesson is not "Do not give your middle school age children marijuana and cocaine in order to encourage them to do their homework" because all my gentle readers have managed to internalize that lesson along with other subtle learning including but not limited to "Don't sit under the apple tree with a pregnant moose on your head" and "Don't stand on one foot in a lightning storm with a metal fork stuck in your eye."

No, the lesson is even more obvious and the lesson is as follows: Do not abnegate your responsibilities as parents, not for a minute, not for any reason, not ever. Eternal vigilance is the price not only of freedom but also of good parenting. Yes, it is easy to motivate children by giving them marijuana and cocaine in order to encourage them to do their homework, but keep your eyes on the prize. Every time it would be easier to sit your child in front of a glowing rectangle so you can consume an alcoholic beverage, THAT IS THE TIME to ask if your daughter would like to give you a hand bathing the dog. Every time it would be easier to do your child's homework FOR him rather than WITH him, THAT IS THE TIME to examine your motivation and ask yourself why it is so important to you that he gets good grades even if--especially if--he is unable to do his homework on his own.

The old English teacher in me can not help but suggest we take a moment away from our regularly scheduled chapter to review some antonyms: The opposite of "teensy-weensy" is "ginormous." The opposite of "look before you leap" is "he who hesitates is lost." And the opposite of children who have half a chance of growing up to be happy and healthy is "giving your middle school age children marijuana and cocaine to encourage them to do their homework." Were we working on synonyms instead, "egregious child abuse" would be the phrase that might spring to mind.

Parenting is hard work. Babies cry in the middle of the night and need to be changed and cuddled when you're exhausted from a long day at work. Preschoolers have frequent come-aparts and need comforting and reassurance that the world is basically a safe place. Middle school kids get out of the car at school only to discover that they have forgotten not only their homework but also their shoes.

Not to mention their science fair project which they mentioned for the first time at 9:00 last night.

But the fact is that you made a deal. When your OB said, "ten centimeters, one more deep cleansing breath then it's time to push, this is it, I can see your baby's head, it won't be long now," you swore that all you wanted was ten fingers and ten toes for your baby. Ten fingers and ten toes and you didn't care if she ever learned to read or went to college. You swore it didn't matter if your child was an accomplished ballerina or pitched the seventh game of the World Series. You swore that if only your baby were healthy you would do the hard work, the 2:00 am feeding, the difficult conversation about reproductive biology, the car pool to the mall with those obnoxious pimply faced kids from down the block who talk too loudly and never shut up and keep saying "like" and "you know" as if those phrases meant anything. You swore you would do whatever it took for as long as it took if only your about to be born child had ten perfect little fingers and ten flawless little toes.

And I didn't make that up; I couldn't make that up. Because your commitment to your kids is truer than true. Truer than the summer rain, truer than the day you met your life time partner, truer than anything that has ever happened on this non-descript, blue-green rocky planet for the past four and a half billion years. And a deal is a deal and you can't quit now. There are no "do-overs" in the game of parenting.

You can continue to fulfill your part of the bargain by not giving your middle school children marijuana and cocaine in order to

144

encourage them to do their homework. You can follow up by modeling sober, ethical behavior and by taking the proper but more difficult course throughout every long day in the lives of your beloved children.

Because a deal is a deal.

My Son the Doctor

"You care for nothing but shooting, dogs and rat-catching and you will be a disgrace, to yourself and all your family."

Ouch!

Can the disappointed father speaking above be excused for his remark? To our modern day sensibility he certainly sounds like his love for his son is anything but unconditional. Indeed, the father comes off as not only disheartened, but also vicious.

What could cause a father to make such a mean-spirited remark? It is hard to read, "you will be a disgrace to yourself and all your family" as supportive and nurturing. It seems unlikely that this father hoping to evoke positive change in his son.

Would you be more sympathetic if you knew that dad had just learned that his son had been deceiving him?
Here's some more of the story to help you decide whether the above remarks were helpful or harsh, merited or unwarranted.

The son to whom the angry father is speaking has just come home from Edinburgh where, as it turns out, he had NOT been studying medicine for the past two years. The young man had instead been hanging out with a zoologist, dissecting not cadavers but marine animals, looking not at human cells under the microscope but at seaweed.

The young man was terrified to communicate to his dad that he just wasn't cut out to study medicine or to be a doctor. He put off the disclosure as long as he could. When the time came and the secret could no longer be kept, the young man admitted that he was not studying medicine and would not study medicine. The father was outraged and suggested that his son's passions extended only to dogs and rat catching.

What happened subsequently to the young man is better known. There were some family resources. The young man's father was a prosperous doctor and his mother's side had some money from their connection to Wedgwood china. Indeed, the young man's mother was a Wedgwood. So, without the blessing of his father, the young man went to sea.

Perhaps you have heard of the young man whose doctor father predicted he would be "a disgrace to yourself and all your family." His interest in zoology persisted on the five-year voyage of the 90-foot sailing ship that left England in 1831. It is unlikely that you know anything about the father, Robert Darwin, the disappointed doctor. But you probable have heard of his son Charles, whose legacy is fairly well regarded in some circles. It is my understanding that the young man's name still comes up in college courses from time to time.

***

So let's get on the right side of history on this one, shall we?

There never has been and there never will be a parade through town for parents who communicated that their children just didn't measure up. Go to the post office and look through all the stamps. You won't find one that says, "My kids weren't who I wanted them to be so I told them to get out." No engraving beneath a statue in the park proclaims, "I thought my children were worthless little shits and I told them so."

Can you imagine our world without our understanding of natural selection? Life saving antibiotics are a direct consequence of our insight into how organisms change. Without Darwin's Origin of Species, there might be even more folks who believe that the Earth came into being some 6000 years ago with civilizations and people already on it. It would be hard to exaggerate the influence of Charles Darwin on civilization.

Can you imagine our world had Robert Darwin been successful in trying to change his son? Can you imagine a world in which Charles Darwin had been forced to be a doctor?

***

148

I am indebted to Carl Zimmer, Stephen Jay Gould, and <u>Evolution: The Triumph of an Idea</u> to which any cogent ideas in this essay may be attributed.

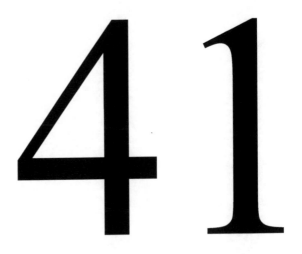

Is This The Person To Whom I'm Speaking

In a conversation with an attorney, I was recently mistaken for my dad who has practiced law in this town for something over half a century. An honest mistake in that my dad and I sound alike on the phone and neither of us had met the attorney in person before this particular conversation. The discussion, such as it was, involved contractual arrangements, amortization schedules, and something apparently called a "prepayment penalty."

Not only was I unaware of the answers, I didn't much understand the questions. I suppose I could have pretended to be an attorney, but the deception would have proved uncomfortable and short-lived because, stop me if I mentioned this point earlier in this paragraph, I had no earthly idea what was being talked about. Thank goodness I was able to disclose that I am not now, nor have I ever been, an attorney. The mistake exposed, the actual attorney and I had a good laugh; he went off to find my dad to chat amicably about title insurance, and I was able to go have a little lie-down.

Imagine though if I had not been able to say proudly, "Hey! I help kids and families make decisions about colleges or therapeutic boarding schools. I do not know an escrow account from a Count Chocula!"

Which is basically what gay people had to do until recently, don't you think? Lie about who they were, I mean. I am not familiar with research regarding a relationship between sexual orientation and breakfast cereal. Before a gay man could say, "No, thank you. I appreciate your willingness to set me up with your offspring, but I'm not interested," he had to say, "Yes, please. I'll look forward to her call." Truly, I don't know what people did in the years before caller ID.

But of course, my books are not about sexual preference, a topic that is right up there with closing statements on the list of things about which I know next to nothing. My books are about children and parenting. So tell me if there might be an analogy here: "My child is smart but lazy. If she just studied harder, she would do better in school." Doesn't that sound just like "Being gay is just a phase. He'll outgrow it. That's not really who my son is"? This parental lament applies to both kids who aren't great students and to gay young people: "They're not who **they** say they are; they are who **I** say they are."

Which is a problem, you have to admit, because wouldn't you agree that the young person with the best insight into who a young person actually is would be said young person rather than some other person even a well-intentioned person of the parental persuasion?

As recently as a hundred years ago, we marginalized, punished, and imprisoned gay people for being who they were. Are you trying to insist that your child is someone else? Are you willing to be angry and disappointed for the rest of your life if your kid doesn't do as well as you would like in school?

What if her "laziness" is neurological? What if she's just not motivated or interested? What if there's something else going on? Sure, she could study harder. In the same sense that my gay cousin could "try" to be attracted to women. But no matter how hard you coerce, cajole, punish, reward, beg, berate, and badger, she still isn't going to take advanced calculus and do well. In the same way that some years ago, someone offered to pick up the dinner check if my cousin would only agree to take a girl to the restaurant.

Which is not to say that we shouldn't encourage our children to do well in their studies, to be intellectually curious, to read widely and well, to talk about ideas, to think critically about subjects both in the classroom and out, to do the best they can in school. Gentle encouragement and modeling are good ideas neither of which ever makes use of sledgehammers.

What you can't do successfully is force your musical child to study accounting or your language-impaired child to be a linguist.

What you can do is destroy your relationship with your son or daughter. Instead of going camping, taking a walk at sunset, hanging out at the dog park, playing Parcheesi, watching "Modern Family," attending a sporting event, tossing a Frisbee, or having a pleasant relationship, you can have each and every conversation go back to the same worn out place: why aren't you somebody else?

152

Throw in a pinch of thinly disguised disgust at the "choices" your child has made and you have the recipe for sadness that can last a lifetime.

42

Game, Set, Match

The 300th best tennis player in the world is so much better than you are at tennis that it is hard to articulate the difference in ability. His *second* serve is consistently over 90 mph; his understanding of strategy is voluminous. Were you to play a match against the 300th best tennis player in the world, there is no chance that you would win one game never mind an entire set. It is unlikely that you would score even one point. There is no doubt but that you would lose 6-0, 6-0, 6-0.

If you were lucky.

The 300th best tennis player in the world was far and away the best tennis player in his high school, the best tennis player in the city in which he grew up, and very likely the best tennis player on his college team. He has a box full of trophies from tournaments all over the country. He is a tremendous athlete.

Yet for all his skill, for all devotion to practice, for all his years of play, the 300th best tennis player on the planet Earth does not make a living from playing tournament tennis. On a given day, he might take a set from the 200th best tennis player in the world. He might even win many of his service games against Roger Federer or Novak Djokovic, were he to somehow participate in a major international tournament against the best of the best, but he bears the expense for his shoes, rackets, and gear. No corporate sponsor or shoe company is paying for his plane tickets to tournaments. If the 300th best tennis player in the world is working in tennis at all, it is as the tennis pro at a country club in a small town in the Midwest. His modest salary pays for his apartment, but if he wants to get married, buy a house, and have children, he is going to have to think about another career.

Certainly there is nothing wrong with earning an honest living doing that which you love: what could be better than getting paid for playing tennis? But if the goal originally was spotlight, fame, millions of dollars and an exorbitant lifestyle, then it must be acknowledged that the fame train has left the station.

The likelihood that the 300th best tennis player in the world becomes number one is something under one in 300. The Number One tennis player in the world did not achieve that ranking by losing to number 300.

A similar argument can be made for the best actress in your child's school, the best violinist, the best writer, the best ballerina, the best photographer, the best artist, the best anything.

Indeed, the number of activities from which your children can make a life but cannot make a living is almost endless: how many working ballerinas do you know?

Here's a riddle: What's the difference between a drummer and a park bench
A park bench can support a family of four

You know the Heisman Trophy, the award for the best player in college football in a given year? There have been 77 recipients since inception. Of whom 15 never played a down in the NFL. There is a 20 % chance that the best player in all of college football in a given year doesn't even get drafted.

Your child therefore had better enjoy soccer, singing, ballet, trombone, karate, or drawing. This essay is not a screed against following a passion for the liberal arts, athletics, or fine arts. This article is an admonition against thinking that your child is going to make a living from being the best at something. Chances are she's not going to be the best. Lots of tennis players. Only one of whom is the best.

I love my running group, the conversation, the camaraderie, the health benefits. But I am not waiting by the phone for someone to offer me free running shoes and a $50,000 appearance fee to run the New York Marathon, an event in which I might finish 27,000th out of 40,000 entrants.

Most people do not have reality shows dedicated to their brutal extravagances. If your children are likely to lead lives not of quiet desperation but just of quiet living--going to work, finding

156

happiness and contentment where they can--why are you setting them up for the almost invariable disappointment of not being the absolute best at tennis or tuba? A more sensible goal, that of doing the best you can and enjoying the journey win or lose, is much more likely to lead to every good outcome.

Given how staggeringly unlikely it is that your offspring is the next Ludwig Van, doesn't shouting, bribing, or being grouchy with your child about piano lessons seems a tragic expenditure of happiness? Doesn't helping prepare your child to be content rather than number one make statistical as well as emotional sense?

43

Questions

Villagers rush to the side of a man with an arrow in his heart who lies bleeding and gasping on a dusty path. "Who shot him?" inquires the first man to arrive at the shaking body.

"Do you think there was an argument?" asks the second.

"Of course there must have been an argument," says a third. "Otherwise, why would he have been shot?"

"What do you think the argument was about?" asked the first man.

As the villagers pause to consider this question, the man on the ground tries to say something, but is interrupted by a fourth villager who says, "I imagine there was money involved,"

"The man who shot him must have been wealthy," advocates a fifth. "Look how beautiful the feathers are on those arrows, probably from a peacock or other expensive bird. Did I ever tell you about the time my cousin was shopping in the next village and wanted to buy some peacock feathers for my niece's second son? Not my niece who married the rock farmer, but my other niece--the one whose left leg was shorter than her right. She was at the local school learning how to combine dirt and water when she thought a cow tried to proposition her. She would never say which cow. So, one day..."

I have too much respect for my gentle readers to subject them to any more dialogue about the family of the fifth villager. Because I know what you're thinking: these people need to stop talking about what the arrows were made out of or the recipe for mud and get to work saving the life of the person who lies bleeding and gasping by the side of the path.

Listening to a mother and father talk about their son Donald's failing grade in math the other day reminded me of the modified Buddhist story above. "If only we weren't getting divorced," Donald's father begins.

"If only you hadn't had an affair with that tootsie in your office," counters Donald's mom.

"Well, if you were more available to take care of your family instead of working all the time," replies dad.

"You know very well Donald did better in math before you moved in with the bimbo," continues mom.

"Do you want me to move back in, is that what you want?" replies dad.

"Donald's math teacher in seventh grade was terrible." mom says.

"At least we can agree on that," dad replies. "She never even graded the homework."

"If only we had sent him to that math camp after elementary school, then everything would be different," says mom.

"You know very well that I am the one who found that program and was in favor of it from the start. It was your mother who said that..."

And off they go, spouting interminable nonsense about that which cannot be changed and makes no difference. As long as his parents keep arguing, that which actually matters-homework, the quadratic formula, getting help from the teacher after school, forming a study group, graphing quadratics, hiring a tutor-goes unremarked upon.

And Donald meanwhile, about whom the conversation was ostensibly concerned to begin with, continues to lie bleeding by the side of the path.

The Expanded Smoking Section

Not the least of the problems with the "smoking section" in airplanes was that the smoke did not pay attention and remain behind row 16 as instructed. As has often been remarked, there is just no talking to some people. The carcinogens in the cigarette smoke did not behave.

And don't even get me started about that guy who promises only to pee on his side of the pool.

Smoke and urine may not pay attention, but parents do. Loving adults everywhere have embraced diversity by sexual orientation, race, social class, and country of origin. Those who have not yet accepted that "they" are quite similar to "we" had better hurry up and get on the bus.

But what about neighbors who put your children at risk? No one's child was ever harmed by a rousing discussion of political events. The same cannot be said for those neighbors who have, for example, unlocked weapons, alcohol, or violent pornography accessible when your nine-year-old goes down the street for a play date after school. It's one thing to have a loud conversation about guns. It's another kettle of bullets altogether to leave guns where kids can get them.

The former are called opinions; the latter are called crimes.

The question is not whether or not your neighbors should keep their guns locked up where kids can't get them. The question is how you find out whether or not they do.

And this information is needed BEFORE any conversation of milk, cookies, or current events.

It requires little effort to keep your children safe from an idea. More corrective action is required for exposure to a bullet traveling at 1700 miles per hour

What about families who allow their middle school children to watch violent pornography WHILE playing with guns AND drinking vodka from the bottle? That drinking vodka straight from the bottle rather than using those attractive little shot glasses is so NOCD (Not Our Class, Dear) is the least of our issues.

162

Do you think that my example is too extreme? Do you think that there aren't any families in your neighborhood who would cause your children harm? Do you feel strongly that there aren't any families at your child's middle school whose worldview would cause irrevocable damage to your beloved children.

Then let's change the conversation from unlocked guns to child abuse and illegal drugs. Do you think that the illegal and deadly drugs are introduced by a stranger from the wrong side of town? Think again. Child abusers are unlikely to be strangers. The bad guy in the black sedan with a lollipop is an urban myth like the alligator in the sewer. The person who is going to introduce your child to recreational narcotics is someone whom your child knows and trusts. Just as the person who wants to abuse your child is someone your child knows, the person who recommends that your child smoke pot is also known to your child. Chances are, the person is someone whom you invited into your home or to whose home you allowed your child to go. Few kids step off the crosstown bus and exclaim, "Howdy! Is there anyone here who would be kind enough to sell me some illegal drugs?"

I don't pretend to have all the answers about how to keep our kids safe. Surely, we have to allow them to go out and experience the world and go for a swim at the home of neighbors. But part of keeping our kids safe might involve making OUR homes the ones where the kids want to come. Board games, cookie recipes, and a relaxed attitude about muddy floors might be a place to start.

Because the bad guys, like carcinogenic cigarette smoke and urine, just don't behave like they're supposed to.

45

Objects at Rest

Whether or not Isaac Newton ever met your Aunt Millie from Topeka is an open question to be debated by historical scholars with more sophisticated research tools than those available to this poor author. Newton was born in 1643. Wasn't that the year in which your mom's sister was graduated from high school?

Whether or not Isaac was thinking about Millicent when he came up with his first law of motion remains to be determined. We do know unequivocally that your aunt binge watches game shows and that she seldom gets up off the couch. When Newton determined that "objects at rest tend to stay at rest; objects in motion tend to stay in motion" was he thinking of her?

You know what else-in addition to your aunt-tends to stay at rest? Students who are supposed to be writing college application essays. Students who are supposed to be writing college application essays stay at rest in a way that makes your lethargic Aunt Millie look like a Ping-Pong ball in a hurricane by comparison.

Students don't start writing, don't start thinking, don't start homeworking unless acted upon. (And yes, I made up the word "homeworking". If I can invent a 400 year-old woman who lived in a city at a time in which there were no Europeans for miles, surely I can invent a word).

This time of year, with college application essay deadlines looming like an anvil heading toward Wile E. Coyote, students are having trouble shedding the inertia and getting started. They stare blankly at blank computer screens thinking about how to. Write. The. First. Word. Of. The. Essay.

"Some students have a background, identity, interest, or talent that is so meaningful they believe their application would be incomplete without it. If this sounds like you, then please share your story."

"Background?" students ask. "*Background*? My mom is from New Jersey. I'm from New Jersey. Everyone in my school is from New Jersey. I don't have a meaningful background. I don't even think New Jersey *is* a background. New Jersey is certainly not meaningful."

"Are there any other choices for essay prompts? Yes, thank goodness. Here is another one: "The lessons we take from failure can be fundamental to later success. Recount an incident or time when you experienced failure. How did it affect you, and what did you learn from the experience?"

"Failure? That's easy. I am failing on my New Jersey butt to come up with a topic for this essay. I'm going to go get a sandwich and return some texts. I'll come back to this in ten minutes."

But, as is so frequently the case, ten minutes becomes ten weeks. And the essays get written--panicked and poorly--at the last possible minute before the deadline.

The antidote to essay inertia is a similar answer to "What do you do to a cookie that is too big to eat all at once?" Answer: "Break it up into small pieces" and "Just get started writing SOMETHING!"

Because writing is hard, but editing is easy. Because there is no such thing as good writing, but there is such a thing as good re-writing. Because perfect is the enemy of good. Because "don't get it right, just get it written" is the only way to overcome inertia.

Even your Aunt Millie from Topeka who has been sitting on the couch for 400 years knows that.

46

It's Not You, It's Them

It would be hard to overstate the carnage resulting from the Corvette drag racing down US 1 at over 100 miles per hour slashing through the Chevette turning left on 17th Avenue. Drivers coming upon the destruction assumed that the fire fighters had cut the Chevette in two in order to remove the occupants. But the fire fighters hadn't even arrived yet and there were no survivors in the Chevette. All three teenagers were dead. The Chevette had been cut in half by the explosive impact, the separate pieces blown apart from each other. The driver of the Corvette was saved by the airbag; his passenger remains a quadriplegic 20 years after the "accident".

Much was written at the time about the under age driver of the Corvette: should his parents have helped him to get a driver's license even though he was not of legal driving age? Should his parents have bought him a second Corvette when he wrapped the first one around a telephone pole a few weeks before the incident described above? Should the parents have proclaimed, "He was not to blame... it wasn't my son's fault"?

Then whose fault was it? Three dead kids and another kid who will never walk again. Doesn't it seem like *someone* was at fault? The death and destruction didn't "just happen." An earthquake is something that happens. A car traveling 50 miles over the speed limit is different. If the car accident didn't "just happen," then whose fault was it?

Not mine, I hope you would agree. I was home that night watching my beloved children, aged two and three, sleep snuggled in their jammies and the panda slippers that they didn't take off except to bathe until they started middle school. Neither was the fault yours, gentle reader.

Since there seems to be enough blame to go around yet no one is at fault, let us turn our attention to the subject of trust. Blame and trust may not occupy the same room, but they certainly live on the same hall. "You don't trust me" is a common lament among teenagers.

"I can't believe you want me home by eleven!" a daughter opines. "Don't you remember when you were my age?"

"Of course I remember when I was your age," her father responds. "That's why I want you home by eleven."

Or stated less cleverly: The response to "Don't you trust me?" is, "Of course we trust you; it's *them* we don't trust."

Okay, then we are agreed that we don't want our kids turning left on 17th Avenue at three in the morning. How do we convince our beloved children that we trust them but that we want them home by eleven just the same, that "nothing good happens after midnight"? How do we both convey and inspire trust while accepting that the population out and about in the wee hours of the morning are over represented by police officers, EMTs, and criminals?

By, er, *trusting* our kids would be a good place to start. By trusting them to make little mistakes when they're little, we allow them to develop the good judgment to avoid making big mistakes when they're big. Doing our best not to be an "I told you so" when their little-kid-imperfect-judgment works out the way you knew it would is also a big help.

The other question I always think about is "who benefits?" Imposing a curfew because you had a curfew when you were a kid is about you. Imposing a curfew to punish your kids is also about you. Imposing a curfew because you don't trust your kids to use good judgment means that something is already imperfect with your relationship with your kids. Whereas imposing a curfew because you want to keep your kids safe is about them. Curfews to keep your kids away from the children of parents who have helped their 15-year-old lie to obtain a fraudulent driver's license and buy him one Corvette after another certainly makes sense to me.

"It's about the relationship, stupid" a politician might have said. Connection, alignment, and attunement with your kids lessens the likelihood of tragedy.

Because you just don't want your kids out at three in the morning. Trust me on that one.

All Kinds of Fun

Let's ignore "fun now and fun later." Catching that big bass with
your grandchild at that sparkling, secluded spot on that perfect fall
day was exquisite at the time and only gets better with each re-
telling. "Say the part again about how the fishing pole almost broke,
Papa. Tell about how nobody could believe a nine-year-old could
catch a fish that big all by himself." Even when you were "in the

moment," you knew the enjoyment would only exponentiate over the years.

"No fun now and no fun later" is hardly worth writing about either. Examples abound: the 90 minute traffic delay that caused you to be late for that third interview and lose the great job, the painful operation that turned out to be unnecessary and unsuccessful.

No, the two categories worth contrasting are:

1) No fun at the time but enjoyable in retrospect.

And

2) Fun at the time but no fun later.

Included in the first category--"A tricky bit of business at the time, but a story on which you can dine out for years"--are camping trips and ultra distance events. "Sure, we didn't have much food left, all our clothes were wet, and we had been abjectly lost for 12 hours, but we didn't die and the first responders were great." And "Yeah, mile 20 was pretty bleak but like I always say, 'if you don't need IV fluids at the end of the event, you didn't run hard enough.'"

Another example of "no fun at the time but fun later": Being lost in the woods when you and your children are cold, wet, and hungry is a lot more pleasant to talk about when you are found, warm, dry, and fed. Wordsworth referred to poetry as "emotion recollected in tranquility" but he could just as easily have been talking about the camping trip where your young daughter was on the trail between those cute bear cubs and their 350-pound mother well known throughout the forest for having no sense of humor where her children are concerned.

Moving on to the last category: The quintessential example of "fun now, no fun later" is recreational drug use. IV drugs are said to be enjoyable for hours after the needle goes in. Crack cocaine is purported to give a pleasant high for a period of several minutes. Later, not so much. Indeed, the greatest misery of addiction recovery is detox and putting a life back together. Stated another way: do you know any active IV drug users living contented lives, providing for their children, planning for their future?

Neither do I.

Structuring our lives to shade toward "no fun now, but fun later" rather than "fun now, no fun later" is where addicts differ from non-addicts. Non-addicts can appreciate delayed gratification. Addicts typically don't even understand the concept.

Visiting an over-18 program in Utah the other day, I had lunch with "Robert" a recovering addict who had been clean for 12 years and "James" who hadn't used for 12 days--including five in detox. Robert was employed as a therapist at the program; James was one of his new clients.

Robert spoke matter-of-factly about a three day mountain bike trip. "Much of the road had been washed away by the flash floods, so we had to walk the bikes up the muddy trails. It took over an hour to cover each mile and we were drenched and exhausted, but the rain stopped just as we got to the top of the range and the vista of the sunset was extraordinary."

"Couldn't you have just driven in a dry car to the same spot to see the same view? "James asked.

James doesn't yet appreciate "no fun now, fun later." He will have to find meaning in his here and now, if he is to have a shot at a future.

Delayed gratification is not about punishing children. "No fun now, fun later" is not about doing things the old-fashioned way. Saving for a rainy day presages studying today and relaxing tomorrow. It's

172

about learning how to pay the mortgage and save for retirement. Not to put too fine a point on it, but internalizing "no fun now, fun later" is about helping your children model the behavior that is less likely to lead to a life destroyed by recreational drugs.

48

Pay Up

Another of my middle aged, balding, paunchy buddies was getting along fine with his girlfriend, getting serious after two years of dating. They were chatting amicably about which caterer to use, making lists of which old friends to invite to the ceremony. Since they were both divorced with grown kids, there was no terrible hurry for them to purchase a home and they certainly wanted to get it right this time. They were spending a couple weekends each month looking at real estate. They liked the same neighborhoods, had the same taste, enjoyed the same features. What could be go wrong? Until my buddy made what turned out to be a blunder of Edsel-like proportions, a Chernobyl-level, five-alarm, screaming screw up.

He mentioned that he had gotten an equity pop when he sold his first house. He told his potential life partner that he had four hundred thousand dollars in the bank.

What had been a pleasant house hunt between equals with similar goals became an epic argument of unrelenting virulence. "Of course, YOU could afford to live in this home" his soon to be ex-fiancé would begin. At the next home she would mumble, "I could afford my half of this house. If I had four hundred thousand dollars."

Within three weeks they were both back on computer dating sites. When they happen to run into one another, they nod politely but do not speak.

Maybe their relationship was doomed from the start. Maybe my buddy should have kept his mouth shut about the money. Maybe he should have spoken up sooner. Maybe there was a way for him to explain that his partner was welcome to the benefits of his good fortune. Or maybe they're just better off moving on. Beats me. I'm no expert on marriage.

But I am supposed to know something about how to raise healthy kids in this careening culture. Therefore, I'm going to make a suggestion about your finances and your kids.

That we live in a society of excess and broken values is not news. Frenzied adults equate expenditures with happiness. Young kids whine about designer backpacks and endorsed shoes. I'm going to suggest that there was something fundamentally wrong with the union of the two disappointed folks described above. Similarly, kids whose emotional needs are being met are less likely to pitch a

175

boogie about acquisitions. Kids who feel misunderstood and disconnected may be looking for material goods to fill the gap.

Not to be overly simplistic, but imagine two middle school kids: Susie has just spent three days canoeing with her dad, sleeping by the river, keeping an eye out for red-tailed hawks, making and eating s'mores every night by the campfire. She has listened spell bound as her father has told her stories about how to survive in the woods. Mary has sat in front of the Disney channel for an equivalent amount of time, texting her friends, absorbing commercials while her parents are elsewhere. Which child is more likely to feel that her needs can be better met by buying something?

Could we go so far as to say that when a child says, "I want a seven-dollar lollipop" what she is actually asking for is something else entirely?

49

Take Them At Their Word

Your Aunt Elizabeth started showing signs of dementia not so many years ago, around her 80th birthday. Her cognitive decline has been as inexorable as it has been painful to watch. Even a year ago she could come up with your name--after running through the list of her deceased husband, all of her sons, and a number of your cousins. Now she just stares blankly, unaware of who you are of why you have come to chat with her. When you introduce yourself, she nods meekly. But five minutes later it is clear she doesn't know how you're related or that you have come to visit every Sunday afternoon for the past two years.

As poignant as it is that the woman who held you in her arms when you were an infant can no longer distinguish you from an employee at her facility, you take her at her word. You have never said, "Don't you try to put one over on me, Aunt Bess. You know very well who I am. If you cared more, you'd remember."

Yet well-intentioned parents commit a similar ugly leap of logic when pretending to have insight into their children's cognitive capability. "Don't you try to fool me, young man. I am certain you could get an A in calculus if only you wanted to."

Maybe. Let's follow both possibilities and consider the risks and rewards.

Suppose your boy COULD study harder, be more productive and organized, learn more proofs, get a better grade. Then gentle encouragement might convey, "I believe in you, I want what's best for you." Just so the message isn't "I love you for what you accomplish rather than who you are," you are on firm parenting ground.

But consider the other, admittedly slippery, side of the street. Your son could hear, "My parents don't know who I am or don't care. They think I'm this math whiz. We are not aligned. We are not attuned." And there is an even worse possibility: "my parents don't listen to me; why should I listen to them?"

Last year over a thousand college students killed themselves. Add the number of young adults dead from drug overdoses and the enormity of preventable deaths becomes brutally apparent.

People talk about a lenient and overindulgent parenting style correlating to kids who become addicted to drugs. But what I see to the contrary is over-controlling pressurized parents forcing their kids to, say, over-perform in college. Stress and pressure can be triggers for students.

For the kids dead of overdoses, drugs were clearly the gun. But I wonder if unrealistic expectations pulled the trigger.

Of course we all want our kids to achieve at the highest level of which they are capable, but if we are going to make a mistake, let's err on the side of staying connected to our kids, letting them speak their truth, and taking them at their word.

Your aunt Elizabeth would feed herself if she remembered how to do so. Your son would perform better in mathematics if he were able. No amount of invective will make a happy difference in either case. You trust your Aunt Elizabeth and she doesn't even remember who you are. Surely, you can be similarly gracious with your beloved children

50

Go Outside and Play

Surely a case could be made for Muhammad Ali, Babe Ruth, Jesse Owens, Wayne Gretzky, Jack Nicklaus, or Michael Jordan as the greatest male athlete of the 20th century. But no vociferous barfly could overlook Jim Thorpe without being asked to step outside and settle the issue. Olympic gold medalist in the pentathlon and decathlon, professional football, basketball, AND baseball player,

180

the man was extraordinary by any standard. Yet there was one athletic effort in which the legendary Thorpe failed.

Thorpe was asked to follow a nine-year-old and mimic his movements: run when the nine-year-old ran, jump when the nine-year-old jumped, swim when the nine-year-old swam, roll down the hill over the rocks into the pond when the nine-year-old rolled down the hill over the rocks into the pond. There is no record of whether or not Thorpe was required to explain to the nine-year-old why using the words "cat," "ceiling fan," and "duct tape" in the same sentence would not be mommy's first choice or how many times he had to repeat this admonition if so. The point is that Thorpe failed to keep up with the nine-year-old. Thorpe gave up, exhausted.

What can loving parents learn from the fact that not even the 20th century's best male athlete can keep up with the unrelenting Super Nova energy of your garden variety nine-year-old?

1) Go outside and play.

No more powerful words were ever spoken by a parent hoping to remain unencumbered by our country's crowded mental health or criminal justice systems. What's that? Where you live there is no place where your kids can safely go outside and play? Here is some directed advice: Move. Quit your job. Sell your house. Move somewhere where your kids can go outside and play.

2) Have some fun with your kids. Toss a ball, go for a swim, take a walk. Then go have a little lie down. Who do you think you are, Jim Thorpe?

3) But if you do consistently drag your out-of-shape, sprained, and sore self down to the park to toss a ball with your kid, keep in mind that backache now can prevent heartache later.

4) Someone pointed out that landed gentry in 19th century Britain did not speak to their children until the kids came back from boarding school at age 16 never mind toss a ball with them. I would mention to this someone that look what has happened to the British Empire in the past century or two and that the last thing you want is children saying "car park" when they obviously mean "parking lot" and asking you to pop round to the "apothecary" when everyone knows they just want something from the drugstore.

In closing, I feel obligated to point out that the story about Jim Thorpe and the nine-year-old may be apocryphal, that is someone may have made it up. That someone might be my dad. Who used to tell me stories, made up and otherwise, when we were tossing the ball together when I was growing up

51

The Greatest Teacher of All

Recently a number of my gentle readers including some number of my own children have made the wildly unsettling allegation that this author's advice to parents trying to raise healthy children in our toxic world can be summed up by the phrase "take the kids camping."

Surely, there is more to adequate parenting in these tough times than just sleeping under the stars, tree roots poking into your neck, in close proximity to raccoon poop. And I would quote journaled research articles from reputable publications supporting this point if only I could find a pencil.

So, rather than do any actual productive work, I will just state: camping is good for kids because the consequences of their imperfect executive functioning and blundering decision making are both humbling and immediately apparent.

Forget to bring enough water on a camping trip, for example, and there is a real problem in real time. Before you can say "consequences for actions" never mind "whose desiccated body parts are these strewn about the trail?" you can feel strongly that your children should have paid attention to the one gallon per person per day rule. Whereas in the city, consequences are neither immediate nor meaningful. Sure, you can step in front of a crosstown bus and get smushed but who does that? A rattlesnake is more subtle and, pound for pound, more instructive.

Are the thoughtful, generous, pleasant people you meet hiking and at campgrounds at glorious National Parks out west nicer than the mean-spirited, snarky, wretched folks who routinely try to steal your hubcaps or sell you stock tips in the city?

To answer this unbiased and imminently reasonable question, consider the following scenario: on a camping trip in the North Georgia mountains some years ago, my sons and I had forgotten to bring an ax with which to chop firewood and were therefore having trouble getting the campfire going. We had a pleasant conversation with some folks from a neighboring campsite, borrowed their ax, made a fire, and ate s'mores until melted marshmallows ran out of our ears and noses. Not an endearing sight admittedly, but ask to borrow an ax from someone on the street in New York City and you get nothing but funny looks.

Family camping trips also engender unforgettable moments. Not all of which need to be processed with a qualified mental health professional in subsequent years. "Remember the time when we ran out of food on that primitive hike 40 miles from the nearest inhabitation and we had to eat berries and dirt for three days?"

"When a man is to be hanged in the morning, it concentrates the mind wonderfully" Dr. Johnson said. Without a signal, your children's electronic devices won't work. A camping trip might, thereby, force you all to have a pleasant conversation about firewood, rattlesnakes, or raccoon poop. Maybe that's all there is to raising healthy kids in a world filled with drugs, violent video games, and crosstown buses.

52

Learning To Read, Reading to Learn

Which child do you think is more likely to become a lifelong learner and love reading until the day he heads up to that big bookstore in the sky?

a) The child for whom reading is an unending series of tedious worksheets followed by vacuous questions or the form "Which of the following statements would the author be most likely to agree?"

b) The kid who cuddles up with his dad on the couch and reads "Spider-Man" comics for hours until father and son get into a raucous squabble about whether the Fantastic Four could have beaten the Avengers so they go out in the backyard and play one-on-one soccer until the ball gets stuck going back and forth between their legs a mile a minute and they both start laughing irrepressibly for no reason to the point where they both fall on the ground howling with the hilarity of it all and the boy says, "It's funny how much fun this is, huh, dad?" and before you tell me that children need to practice for standardized tests because there are college admission exams in their future, let me hasten to remind you that there are unspeakable medical procedures in your future but I don't see you drinking that gallon of horrific pineapple-flavored liquid for *"practice"* and yes, I am quite aware that this sentence is a run-on, but you take my point.

Because as my grandmother often remarked, "You're a long time dead.

Before we shuffle off this mortal coil, shouldn't we have some connections with our kids? Some years hence, when you're drooling into your napkin at the assisted living facility, don't you want to be thinking back on the comic books, the one-on-one soccer, and the disputation on Reed Richards versus Tony Stark as the most brilliant inventor in the comic book universe?

Or stated another way, where do the memories come from?

Remember the time your nine-year-old son was exhausted from a long day at school and lacrosse practice and just wanted to cuddle up with you on the couch and hear a made-up story about dinosaurs or astronauts but instead you reminded him that he had worksheets to do for homework?

Nah. Probably not.

The hours spent reading comic books on the couch and the one-on-one soccer games are emblazoned in memory. The worksheets, not so much.

We all want our kids to be able to read. The question is how we help them to acquire the skill. Just like a man who loves his job will never work a day in his life, a child who loves learning will more likely be able to study the requisite 14 hours a day necessary to score well enough on the Medical College Admissions Test to become a doctor. The child who has only been exposed to "passages" who has never chosen a book just for the sheer joy of finding out WHAT HAPPENS NEXT?! Again, not so much.

After 37 years of teaching and counseling kids and parents, I am convinced that an afternoon spent reading that which is intrinsically interesting beats the heck out of not paying any attention to enforced curriculum.

You could argue that the kids who love the infinitely intricate plots and wonderfully stable characters of Harry Potter are more likely to be successful in the classroom. I would argue that questions of the form "In line 237, 'vicissitude' most closely means which of the following?" make me want to hurry out behind the barn and bury all testing material.

I would replace "three-minute record" in Springsteen's, "we learned more from a three-minute record, baby, than we ever learned in school" with "Spider-man #33." The plots of those comics can lead directly to Jane Austen and Henry Fielding.

And speaking of Spider-man #33, what happened to all those great comic books I read in the 1960s, those great stories to which I attribute my love of all things literary? Lost tragically, I'm afraid. As it happens, I'm trying to recreate my collection for subsequent generations of Altshulers. If you have old Marvel comic books--

specifically Spider-Man issues from #1 to #83 (about the time in my life when I moved on to more well known forms of literature,) I would be pleased to purchase them from you. Respond to David@Altshulerfamily.com and let's chat.

53

What Do You Want?

Warning: some content may not be appropriate for younger readers. At two o'clock in the morning at a fraternity party, a senior tells a first year student that he has been attracted to her for the entire semester but has never spoken to her until now. He alternates encouraging her to sip vodka with insisting that she drink beer. When the young woman is barely able to stand, he takes her to his room where he removes her clothes.

190

Subsequently, the young man never speaks to the young woman again, avoiding her in class and on campus. Even after she has involved the authorities, the trauma haunts her throughout her life, influencing her every relationship.

Across the quad, a young man and a young woman finish a long walk and a small bottle of wine. They talk about their long-standing mutual attraction and determine to take their relationship to the next level by becoming physically intimate. After chatting about sexually transmitted diseases, reproductive biology, and expectations, they begin a mutually satisfactory series of sleepovers. Years later, they still reflect glowingly on how great their senior year connection was. Subsequent relationships are measured against the standard of the agreeable interaction of senior year.

The purpose of this chapter is not to argue which scenario is more common. Only to suggest that the behavior of the two couples is predicated on what they want-long term and short. Although both narratives intersect with sex, what happened before and after is the difference between felony and romance.

Just as where you sit determines where you stand, your goals as parents define how you handle each interaction with your children. Threats and coercion can enforce short-term compliance, but are unlikely to lead to a long-standing positive relationship.

Consider a four-year-old who would rather play with his Legos than put on his shoes and accompany his dad to the market. A father who aggressively says, "You know how to put on your shoes! I'm going to give your toys away unless you do as you're told" will get a different response than a parent who says, "I know how much you love to play with those Legos. Let me help you with your shoes."

Which interaction will encourage the child to be more likely to put on his shoes by himself next time? Which conversation will allow the child to reciprocate unconditional positive regard for his father? Which will pave the way for a father whose opinions about important topics are respected and valued?

People respond to how we feel about them rather than to how we act with them. (For a more thorough and better explanation of this point, see The Anatomy of Peace.) The angry father may be feeling stressed and hurried. He may be worried that his child is being coddled by his mother-in-law who puts the child's shoes on for him and with whom he disagrees about child rearing. He may be concerned that his child is somehow behind in some imagined race for independence or compliance.

The attuned, sensitive father conveys that his kid is okay and that his son won't walk down the aisle barefoot. Indeed, all developmental milestones will be achieved earlier and more gracefully by children who are grounded, secure, and nurtured rather than those who are coerced, bullied, and threatened. Sure, compulsion works. But are force and deception what you want your relationship with your children to be based on?

If you have trouble answering that question, reread the account of the sexual experience of the girl described in the first paragraph above.

54

Mastodons, Math, Rain Running, and Addiction

Consider Mr. Atrobus versus a mastodon. Atrobus is hungry. But the mastodon does not fancy appearing on anyone's luncheon menu. One on one, the smart money is on Proboscidea.

Because soaking wet, Atrobus tips the scales at something south of 200 pounds, about 10,000 pounds short of your recalcitrant mastodon. Ten millennia later when scales are invented, it's still Apollo Creed versus Glass Joe: the lone human is hopelessly outclassed.

Give Mr. Atrobus a spear. Your bookie still won't take your call.

But give Mr. Atrobus 20 guys and suddenly the odds overwhelmingly favor our starving Homo habilis. So much so that there are now some seven billion of his descendants and none of the mastodon's. The final mastodon caught the last train for the coast 11,000 years ago last Thursday. The cause of this extinction may have had to do with environmental conditions, but the more likely explanation is that Mr. Atrobus and those other guys with the spears learned how to cooperate and hunt in a group. Individuals go hungry; members of a group have a nosh and go on to the maternity ward.

Fast forward through the Pleistocene to a torrential downpour last Saturday morning. Snuggled in my comfy bed at 5:30 when the alarm goes off, I am eagerly allowing myself to go back to sleep. I can run later; I can run tomorrow; I can run never. What difference could it possibly make if I miss one lousy workout?

Except my buddies are waiting for me in the maelstrom at the Area Formally Known as Parrot Jungle. And although I may not care enough about myself to try to stave off my own impending paunchiness, heart disease, and mortality, I will be darned if I allow any of those things to happen to my friends.

So I lace up my shoes and head out into the rainstorm.

In the deluge, maybe our group runs ten miles instead of 15; maybe we run each mile in 10 minutes instead of our usual nine; maybe we use inappropriate language every sentence instead of every other.

194

But we are there for one another as we have been for well over half our lives, as we will continue to be until we limp off to that ultra marathon in the sky. The group is more than the sum of its parts. We run as a group; as individuals we remain supine.

Of course this chapter is not about chomping on mastodons nor dodging raindrops in the dark. It's about helping your beloved children to achieve academically and maximize their potential as learners.

There is an idea in this country that it is preferable for the individual to accomplish on his own, that working together is somehow "cheating". Daniel Boone was said to pull up stakes and move further west whenever he saw smoke coming from another habitation over the hill. This outdated idea of the rugged individual still exists in some families: "he has to learn how to get homework done on his own."

Nah. A more appropriate metaphor is sharing and support. Physics papers are invariably produced collaboratively. The names of 200 authors are more common on a journal publication than is a single scientist. As unlikely as it is for a single hunter to bring down a mastodon, building the $13 billion CERN collider in Switzerland was not a one-person job either.

Or as one of my favorite wilderness therapist pointed out, "if you want to travel fast, travel alone. If you want to travel far, travel together."

If your child is struggling in math, encourage him to set up a consistent meeting time and place with a study buddy. If his motivation is waning, agree to facilitate transportation and popcorn. Ideally, the other student at the library or kitchen table will be someone of comparable ability and in the same math class, but any able-bodied adolescent will be preferable to the unmitigated horror of trying to open the book and get to work on his own. I've heard students in middle school exclaim incredulously, "I can't return a text NOW! My friend is counting on me to help her study."

For addicts in recovery, the paradigm is the same. Nobody savvy about rehab recommends reading 90 books in 90 days. Nobody insists on going on 90 hikes in 90 days. Although reading and the outdoors are powerful teachers, the likelihood of sobriety is enhanced by attending 90 meetings in 90 days. The power to continue clean and sober comes from connecting with others of our species, sharing stories and support. All of us are carrying spears, all of us together bringing down one of the biggest mastodon of all-- addiction.

It has been said that truth is a hard deer to hunt. As part of a group, our odds are significantly better.

55

I Know an Old Woman

I know an old woman who swallowed a fly...

My baby is still colicky after three months. He still does not sleep for more than two hours at a time. All the other mothers I chat with at the gym have babies who are sleeping through the night. Sometimes, I give him a little brandy to help him sleep. And then I take a shot myself.

I don't know why she swallowed a fly...

My five-year-old just will not behave. He is always asking me to do stuff. It is so annoying. He has no appreciation of how tired I am when I get home from work. I gave him an iPad with lots of games, but he still keeps asking me questions and bothering me. Will I read him a story? Will I take him to the park? Will I bounce a ball with him? A ball? Really?

Do I look like a woman who has time to bounce a stupid ball with a five-year-old?

I know an old woman who swallowed a spider.
That wiggled and jiggled and tickled inside her.
She swallowed the spider to catch the fly.
I don't know why she swallowed the fly.
Perhaps she'll die.

My third grader isn't paying attention in school. He won't do the assigned worksheets in class never mind do all the worksheets for homework. Our pediatrician says that my son is just an active child who needs to go out and play but I insisted that we get a prescription for psycho-stimulants. The pediatrician wouldn't prescribe them but I bought some Adderall from one of the moms at the club. It didn't seem to work though--my son is still hyperactive and inattentive--so I added twice daily doses of Ritalin and Vyvanse.

I know an old woman who swallowed a bird.
How absurd. She swallowed a bird.
She swallowed the bird to catch the spider
That wiggled and jiggled and tickled inside her.
She swallowed the spider to catch the fly.
I don't know why she swallowed the fly.
Perhaps she'll die.

Now my son is in ninth grade. He is acting out like you wouldn't believe. He talks back, is totally disrespectful, his grades are terrible, sometimes he cuts school to drink beer and smoke pot with his

198

friends. I took him to a psychiatrist who met with him for six minutes and prescribed an SSRI, Prozac I think it's called. My son doesn't like the medication, says it gives him headaches or some nonsense, but anyway it wasn't working so I doubled the dosage.

I know an old lady who swallowed a cat.
Imagine that. She swallowed a cat.
She swallowed the cat to catch the bird.
How absurd. She swallowed a bird.
She swallowed the bird to catch the spider
That wiggled and jiggled and tickled inside her.
She swallowed the spider to catch the fly.
I don't know why she swallowed the fly.
Perhaps she'll die.

My son is going to turn 18 soon; he is completely out of control. He won't go to school, plays "League of Legends" all day, doesn't speak to me except to ask for money. The SSRIs didn't work so I got him some atypical anti-psychotics and some mood stabilizers. The Abilify doesn't work either. I don't know why I keep going to these idiot doctors. They are no help whatsoever. My son's behavior just gets worse and worse.

I know an old lady who swallowed a goat.
She just opened her throat. And swallowed a goat.
She swallowed the goat to catch the cat.
Imagine that. She swallowed a cat.
She swallowed the cat to catch the bird.
How absurd. She swallowed a bird.
She swallowed the bird to catch the spider
That wiggled and jiggled and tickled inside her.
She swallowed the spider to catch the fly.
I don't know why she swallowed the fly.
Perhaps she'll die.

I haven't heard from my 24-year-old son in over a year. Somebody told me that he was living in California eking out a meager living from dealing the prescription pain pills to which he himself is addicted. I can't imagine how he got involved with illegal drugs. All the drugs I ever gave him were from doctors or other parents.
I know an old lady who swallowed a horse.
She's dead of course.

I would not pretend that just allowing an active child to go outside and play is the surefire, one size fits all cure for all learning differences, attentional issues, and family conflict. Dyslexia, dyscalculia, and dysgraphia are all real. Medications CAN be useful and appropriate.

What I am interested in is the escalating human cost of the alleged psychotropic cures and whether or not less intrusive, more effective alternatives exist. If you would prefer to have a loving relationship with your child, at the very least you must consider involving the child in the decision to imbibe brain-altering chemicals. You might even decide that some things are more important than a child behaving calmly or completing worksheets. Here are two examples of what you might consider to be more important than a calm child completing worksheets: a child who is not completely estranged from his parent; a child who is not suffering from addiction to drugs.

56

ER

After a buddy of mine had the poor judgment to choose to be born on the island of Hispaniola, he compounded his ineptitude 30 years later by contracting malaria. Sensitive to my wife's unyielding policy of "no dead guys in the living room," I drove Sebastian to the county hospital where we learned that 1) a fever of 104.1 does not move you to the front of the line and 2) seven hours in the waiting room is more than enough time to tell every joke you've ever heard and 3) if there is ever a good time to become involved in healthcare in a major metropolitan area, Saturday night during a full moon is not that time.

There were a lot of people in the ER. A lot in the sense that there are "a lot" of stars in the sky. Sebastian was endeavoring to get his fever up over 105 degrees so that he could cut the line and receive medical care before the end of the Pleistocene. I was trying to determine the job descriptions and responsibilities of the various uniformed personnel scurrying about, none of whom seemed to be tasked with engaging with actual patients or providing what might have been termed "care."

One woman, whom I will refer to as "the sitter upper" appeared responsible for ensuring that none of the potential patients--either from hunger, fatigue, boredom, or actual illness--remained face down on the tile floor.

Perhaps there were fire lanes involved as I would suggest that you have attended weddings that weren't as crowded as this cavernous emergency room. You have heard about fraternity parties with fewer supine bodies strewn about every horizontal surface. When I obsequiously responded to "the sitter upper" that Sebastian was too ill to get up off the floor, she replied, "He walked in here, didn't he?"

Point taken.

Let us leave Sebastian's inert and feverish frame slumped over a folding chair (he must have recovered at some point or I would not have been able to leave the hospital to write this book) and consider a different venue. My wife experienced a minor come-apart recently in a small town out west. Dropping her off in the emergency room, I prepared myself for a waiting period equivalent to that required to adopt a child from Central America. But before I could park the car

202

and hurry back into the clean, well-lit facility, my wife was already being attended to by an articulate and compassionate triage nurse. Within moments, eight other medical personnel had poked and prodded, tickled and tested, and provided ultrasound, MRIs, and advice to my stunned spouse.

One of the nurses even went so far as to offer me a soft drink.

The only thing the doctor did not do in one of his four lengthy conversations with my bride was to offer her a foot massage. Whether or not Patti received a mani pedi remains an open question as I dozed off in a comfy chair at one point and can not be certain what transpired during my brief snooze.

That there are differences in the quality of healthcare delivery systems in disparate cities is not news. That it would be cheaper, faster, and more efficient to fly across the country to receive adequate medical attention is worth noting. Even getting through TSA and a four-hour transcontinental flight is more attractive that flopping around on the floor and having your roasting carcass emptied into a chair in the big city waiting room.

Allowing your children to choose the right friends is similar to qualifying for boutique health care. You know those kids who live on the 47-foot boat behind the home of their absent parents, the kids who have no chores or responsibilities, the ones who smoke pot every day before school? Your kids would do well not to spend any time over there. When something bad happens--mortgage the farm, something bad invariably happens when unsupervised 17-year-olds live on a 47-foot boat--it would be well if your kids were elsewhere.

Of course, flying out west every time your buddy decides to contract malaria is as unrealistic as hopping on a flight whenever your kids want to go play. The good news is that whereas malaria befalls an unfortunate, keeping your kids safe from children making absurdly poor choices is easier.

When the kids are little, allow them to choose the friends who play imaginative games and run around outdoors rather than children who are drowning in glowing rectangles. Invite for play dates those kids who understand "we don't do that here" instead of "let's watch another fart video."

When the children are older, take them hiking and camping with peers who don't smoke pot.

Because unlike boutique health care, the good kids are just around the corner. There are families who share your values. You don't even have to travel half way across the country to find them.

57

Right and Wrong

As devoted readers of these chapters will attest, sunshine, lollipops and unicorns have nothing on my opinion of a father-daughter hike on a crisp fall day where the twigs pop under your sneakers, the stream runs cold over the stones, and the panoramic view from the top of the mountain is breath taking. Remembering the sunscreen, bug spray, and PBJs are--like the Swiss flag--a big plus.

Forgetting the first aid kit and the binoculars goes without saying. But what could be better than the shared experience of silently watching a red-tailed hawk fly away with a black snake in her talons? (In the interest of journalistic integrity, I should disclose that my daughters and I have never seen anything of the kind on our rambles. Indeed, we frequently don't see an animal bigger than a mosquito, but the point remains.)

Still, it is possible to get hiking wrong. A forced march filled with instructions--"Look at that tree!"--Interrogations--"Did you make up your math test?--and recriminations--"I hope you appreciate this trip because I have a lot of work I'm missing at the office"--can be miserable. Simple silence can communicate that parents and kids like to spend time together in the outdoors. Whereas a bombastic monologue inhibits introspection and enjoyment. A parent who intones, "Walk faster, there's a more interesting tree up ahead" might as well just stay home in front of the television.

Similarly, it is possible to get the education of children with learning differences horribly, miserably wrong. Blaming children for the way they process information is seldom productive. Marginalizing these kids, punishing them with dumbed down curriculum, attacking them with endless worksheets, and sequestering them away from "normally achieving" students--all are a recipe for poor outcomes.

I toured a school recently that got it right. In another setting, these students with mild to moderate learning differences would have been discarded as unable or unwilling to learn. But with four to eight children in a classroom, infinitely patient teachers, and inspiring curriculum, these kids were absorbing information at 100% of capacity.

In the lunchroom, students and teachers sat together, chatting animatedly and amicably. I sat with the director of admissions, the athletic director, and the head of residential life. Student after student came up to our table, shook my hand, and made polite introductions. "Nice to meet you; where are you from? Thanks for coming to visit."

Really? "Thanks for coming to visit"?

You can't fake that sincerity. Genuine pleasantness in adolescent populations usually known for self-absorption and snarkiness is rare. No amount of preparation can inspire kids to introduce themselves to an adult visitor. These kids were the real deal--active and involved with their educations, connected to the success of their process and their school. "Nice to know you." Wow. Talk about your lollipops and unicorns.

That our culture does not have the resources or the will to provide appropriate education for more than a fraction of our population of school-aged children is the subject of another book.

Was this school a "good" school? Measured by the list of "top" colleges to which their high school graduates matriculate, probably not. None of these kids was going on to get a PhD in philosophy from Princeton. But considered from the standpoint of going on to have productive lives rather than ending up playing video games in basements indefinitely, this institution is top-notch. The vast majority of these kids go on to college. The vast majority of kids with learning differences in other settings don't.

My daughters and I will never win an Olympic medal in the non-existent category of "fastest hike up a mountain with a gurgling brook and a view of the valley," but there is something to be said for the experience none-the-less.

Similarly, shouldn't we all be proponents of helping our children find the best placement, the most appropriate school, the place where they can thrive? Is the occasional rainbow too much to ask?

(Not mentioning the actual name of the school I visited is intentional. I pride myself on not promoting any specific boarding school, college, residential treatment center, product or service of any kind in these chapters. However, if you write to me privately at David@Altshulerfamily.com I will connect you with the school with the wonderful support for students who learn differently.)

58

Publish or Perish

My mom has perfect grammar. She knows who and whom, can tell a dangling participle from a gerund. Wake her up in the middle of the night and she will tell you when to use "ten-year-old" instead of "ten year old." Throw a term paper across the room and, before it hits the floor, my mom will tell you that there should be a semi-colon on page seven.

Not only that, my mom has published the best selling humanities text book in the country. The Art of Being Human is now on its eleventh edition.

When my mom takes a standardized test of written expression, she is finished--every answer correct--before the other students are done chewing on their pencils. "Neither of the girls are having a good time"* screams at my mom the way "The Germans won the Second World War" jumps out at you.

Yet even my mom has an editor.

When she and her co-author, my Uncle Richard, work on the galley proofs of their books, they use a ruler to read **up** the pages. Reading down the page, it's easy to get lost in the content and not find the typos. It's tough to find the errors in your own writing so they go through the book one line at a time.

Your children, I need hardly remind you, are not college English professors with decades of experience correcting thousands of essays. For elementary school aged children, letting them dictate a book can be a great gift. Forget about grammar. Heck, forget about sense for little ones learning to love language. You can write out the words, "Once upon a time, there was a mean dinosaur" and your child can supply the illustrations. The story may have a sophisticated narrative structure and complex character development.

But probably not.

What you're communicating in the collaboration is that you enjoy hanging out with your kid, taking a glorious bubble bath of words. And you're doing something pleasant and productive, making a memory.

Because, although the days are long, the years fly.

Seven-year-olds have a tendency to become 27-year-olds before you can blink. Yesterday they were saying "spasgetti" and "pumpquin". Later this afternoon, they will be grown and gone, their empty bedrooms a stark testimony to the inexorable passage of time.

So what would you rather look back on? The memory of a high score in a violent video game or the tangible product of a sun-kissed afternoon spent making a mess of crayons and tape on the kitchen table and creating a "book" about a lonely bear? The digital footprint of the twenty-seven bazillion points may be more indelible than the fading pages but so what? Just because everyone is still talking about the First World War doesn't mean it was any fun at the time for the participants.

My sister volunteers at the historical society. She says there is little interest in old books, but that her colleagues are eager to collect and study the letters of folks who lived in Massachusetts generations ago. Just as Jane Austen teaches us more about life in the time of Napoleon without ever mentioning a specific current event, correspondence gives us more insight into the moral landscape of a time and place than volumes of print.

Generations from now, I suspect no one will be cataloging high scores from "Frogger" or "Call of Duty", but the legacy you can share with unborn generations is the supernova creativity of your beloved six-year-old bursting out on pages of construction paper. There will be time for vapid essay topics to be forced on your unsuspecting child. In school "prompts" will be supplied on themes upon which no human would wish to expound. Some purveyor of textbooks may inflict hackneyed subjects seemingly designed to quash rather than enhance creative responses. But in the privacy of your own home, you can harness the entire universe as seen through the wide-open eyes of your child.

Here is an offer: If you follow my gentle advice and make an eight-page "book" with your third grader, thirty years from now, I will give you one million dollars for what the two of you created.

I feel completely certain that you will not accept the money, that you won't trade the illustrated fading pages of "The Silly Penguin" for all the money in the world.

PS. Read the words in the triangle again. If you think it says, "I love Paris in the Springtime", read it again and again until you see what it actually says. The word "the" appears twice.

* The subject of a sentence cannot be in a prepositional phrase. "Neither" is singular. "Neither of the girls is having a good time" is correct.

59

Do You Want to Dance

New to the sixth grade and new to the school, my son was pleased to receive an invitation to a dance. "Dance," as it turns out, has more than one meaning of which shy children asking one another to do the twist is not the relevant one. At this country club, 11-year-olds were exhorted to line up by gender, girls in the front, boys in the back. The four disc jockeys, over thunderous bass--and I use the term loosely--"music" encouraged the pre-pubescent boys to grind their pelvises against the tushies of the anonymous--we were all new to the school, remember--girls in front of them.

Let me disclose here that I can hardly be described as a prude. I like to think I have as much libido as the next 59-year-old man. Not that anyone asked me, but I would neither expect nor encourage young adults to be physically intimate for the first time after a walk down the aisle or trip to city hall. Indeed, it is my understanding that my grandmother didn't know where babies came from when she got married. It would be hard to overstate the trauma associated with such events as a wedding night of a hundred years ago. Young people should, in my judgment, know who they are, what they enjoy, what feels good, before committing to monogamy. A young person having her first experience with physical intimacy only after marriage seems, for want of a better phrase, old fashioned and unlikely.

That said, I admit to having felt somewhat awkward as I walked across the expanse of tablecloths, hors d'oeuvres, and mixed drinks to remove my young son from the "dance." I imagine he felt awkward as well being led away to "have a little talk" about "good touch and bad touch" and "ages and stages." Oh, well. It wasn't the highlight of my weekend either. If parenting only included celebrating our children's joys and triumphs, there would be fewer families whose only interaction consisted of a card once a year. The hard job was extricating my son from an event--anonymous sexualized grinding--that may have made him uncomfortable and certainly gave me the creeps.

The question is not whether or not the broader culture is influencing your children. The only question is how you will allow that influence to be felt in your family.

If you're going to say "no," "no, you cannot attend a party with free-flowing vodka but without adult supervision on a 57-foot boat in the canal behind the home of a classmate whose parents have more

214

money than sense," you must also say "yes." "Yes, we are going camping that weekend; yes, you can bring as many friends as you like; yes, we will jump into the spring that is so cold that my bones ache just thinking about it; yes, I will take that Friday off from work; yes, my child is my highest priority; yes, we may be cold, wet, lost and covered with bug bites but we'll laugh about it later and no one will be modeling that it's okay to have simulated sex in public at age 11."

Mortgage the farm: If you do not suggest some values and virtues for your children, your neighbors will be happy to provide theirs.

Did the child whose party is described above wake up one morning and say, "I have an idea! Let's hire four obnoxious adults who will suggest that my 11-year-old male classmates line up and grind their pelvises into the behinds of my 11-year-old female classmates"?

No. She did not. To the contrary, this child would have been happier and better served with almost any other commemoration of the beginning of her twelfth year.

There is some small piece of a happy ending to the over-the-top event described above and the embarrassing extrication of my child. While my son and I were chatting about appropriate behavior and what polite excuse we were going to invent for leaving the party early, we noticed another dad who had also led his child away from the throbbing noise and the simulated sexual intercourse on the dance floor. I can only assume that he and his son were having a similar conversation. I can say that our boys are friends to this day, ten years later.

In some sense, your precious children just ended up living with you. They didn't have any choice in the matter. It is your sacred trust to bring them up the way you want to. To deny their birthright and hand over their upbringing to those who think that unidentified groping is appropriate for young ones is to abnegate your most essential obligation.

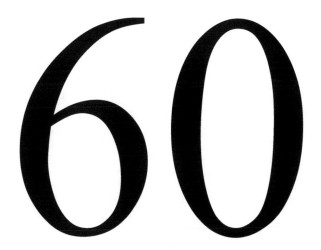

Fun, Fun, Fun!

Some gentle readers who have been with me for 250 of these rabble-rousing musings have had the unmitigated temerity to suggest that my *anti-drug, pro-running, be responsible for your kids* screeds can be summarized as "fun is bad." Not everybody wants to wake up at oh dark hundred, join similarly afflicted loonies, and train for 50 km romps through the swamps after which the most cogent remark is often "another packet of IV glucose solution, please." Surely, there are other ways to fill our brief moments of strutting and fretting across the stage without inflicting more discomfort than that which is inevitably headed our way after the doctor says, "The bad news is that you have a painful, incurable disease; the good news is that I'm sleeping with my receptionist."

To address this dreadful calumny, that I recommend suffering for its own sake, I will only suggest that ordering a $700 bottle of vodka at a South Beach club while listening to records being sawed in half does not work for me. If listening to "Paul is dead" played backwards and a blood alcohol level that would kill a moose works for you and you are able to be at your desk at nine o'clock the next morning then good for you. Not that you asked, but you have my blessing. My concern is only for those for whom this definition of fun leaves them un-launched, sad, addicted, and unconnected-- emerging from their parents' metaphorical basements only to eat Cheetos and borrow the credit card this one last time.

One of the great things about a predilection for distance running is that we always want to stop. One of the not so great things about addiction to oxycontin is that you always want more. See the difference?

Where did all those young people in the treatment programs I visited recently in Arizona and Utah come from? How did they get there? How did their addictions come to control their lives? No one ever woke up in the morning and said, "I have an idea! I will become addicted to Xanax. I will ignore my studies, my family, my children, my responsibilities, and devote my life to the procuring and ingesting substances."

I'm thinking the process was more gradual.

Just as every heart surgeon who does heart transplants once did a heart transplant for the first time (a good thing if a scary one), every

218

chemically dependent young adult once took one pill once for the first time.

The forces of evil are, as always, as clandestine as ever: a respected oral surgeon, with a wink and a nod, gives "extra" painkillers to an adolescent with the suggestion that the young man "have a good time." There seems to be a conspiracy to convince our kids that nothing should ever hurt.

That our kids will never have a bad day seems an unlikely promise to fulfill and an improvident suggestion. The Dread Pirate Roberts summed up this concept in "The Princess Bride": "Life is pain, Highness. Anyone who says differently is selling something."

I am not suggesting that there is anything to be said for needless misery. But an argument can be made for delaying gratification. You don't have to join my running group at 5:45 am to go schlepping and sweating through the fetid swamp to appreciate the joy that comes from not running, but you would do well to allow your children to understand that a little discomfort is to be expected.

If the cross-country team doesn't appeal, a boring after school job would not be the end of the world. Giving your kids Advil rather than Darvocet after a minor procedure might not be a bad idea either. And if you do give your child a narcotic after surgery, throwing away the extra 19 pills could be an important step in avoiding a basement filled with unrealized expectations and Cheetos.

61

The Ouch Paradigm

Ignaz Semmelweis, so history tells us, was the preeminent obstetrician in Europe in the 1840s. Educated, credentialed, and well read, Semmelweis was the Big Kahuna of baby delivery doctors two centuries ago.

Except that the babies he delivered died at a disproportionately higher rate than those delivered by folks who didn't work at the fancy-schmancy hospital.

The babies delivered by midwives who never set foot in the hospital were more likely to survive. The babies delivered by Semmelweis and his staff were significantly more likely to get infected with fevers and die.

Type in "Ignaz Semmelweis" in Wikipedia if you are interested in the numbers and the charts.

How could this be? Semmelweis considered and eliminated every possible factor that could be contributing to the differential mortality. Was one clinic more crowded than the other? Was one clinic colder than the other? Were the religions of the woman in one clinic different from those of the women in the other? There was no difference in any of these factors. What was causing the babies delivered in the hospital to have such bad outcomes?

Semmelweis determined that the doctors in the hospital came into contact with cadavers during their training while the midwives did not. Even though there was no "germ theory of disease" in those days, Semmelweis figured out that he himself was the problem, that he and his staff were transmitting the infections that caused so many babies to die. "Iatrogenic" is defined as "illness cause by medical examination or treatment" by Merriam-Webster but I think of iatrogenic as harm caused by trying to help. Semmelweis instructed his staff to wash their hands after working on their cadavers before delivering babies. Problem solved.

Consider a parent deciding which summer camp her neuro-typical kids should attend. A generation ago, the determination would have been made as follows: "Hey, Liz!" a neighbor would call out across a backyard fence. "What was the name of that summer camp that your cousin's kid went to? You know, the one with the lake!" And that would be the end of it.

Today to the contrary, it is not uncommon for a parent to take off work, get on a plane, and visit half a dozen venues.

Or as one of my running buddies pointed out, "This woman visited six summer camps across the country? I spent less time figuring out which house to buy."

Consider the mother of a fourth grader asking her son's teacher if the math homework had been corrected yet. "No, it was just turned in a few hours ago," the teacher responds.

"Then could I have it back? I want to correct a mistake that I--er, ahem, of course I meant 'he'--made on the second subtraction problem."

The teacher gently suggests that ten-year-olds should be doing their own homework. Oblivious, the mother goes on to ask if she can borrow the key from a different fourth grade teacher. Her intention is to sneak into the classroom, steal the homework, and correct the errant problem.

Before you suggest that both moms described above have "too much time on their hands" and that they are destroying any chance their children might have of growing up independent and responsible, consider the perspective of the moms: They just want to help.

I would not presume to guess what is going on in the mind of the woman traversing the country to count the bathrooms in cabins. Nor would I be so presumptuous as to guess what the homework-stealing mother is thinking. But I wonder if a psychologist might suggest an interior monologue like the following: "See what a good mother I am? See how hard I work to make sure you have every advantage?

See how much time I spend ensuring that everything goes easy for you?"

As long as mom is hyper-involved with controlling every potential bump in her son's life, she doesn't have to consider her own stuff. Maybe her marriage is plagued by infidelity; maybe she has substance abuse issues; maybe she would do well to be looking inward.

But as long as her son is the one who needs care, as long as she has a 'job', there is no reason for her to consider her own concerns. Her son has stubbed his toe, yet mom is the one to say "Ouch!" While she is visiting summer camps and stealing homework, neither mother nor son is likely to experience growth.

Perhaps Ignaz Semmelweis 175 years ago was not the only one doing harm by trying to help.

Loving parents today would do well to consider Winnicott's "good enough parent." Doing too much for our kids can be as harmful as doing too little. We should communicate to our children that ultimately, the responsibility for their finding fulfillment and contentment will be theirs and not ours.

62

Rich and Famous

The year after Kathy retired following three decades of teaching English at the university, she published her fifth novel and ran her tenth marathon. She paid off her mortgage. One early morning as we plodded toward Matheson Hammock to watch the sun rise, she reflected on how keeping score by these milestones left her feeling uneasy and unfulfilled.

"I write with discipline," she opined. "Especially since I stopped teaching. I start every morning at nine, half an hour for lunch, and keep at it until three."

Our group of a dozen sweaty runners stopped telling jokes to listen. Kathy seldom stopped joshing with the rest of our group to speak seriously about her life. "I'm never going to create anything remotely comparable."

"Comparable to what?" Elena asked.

Kathy half recited, half sang:

'Now the years are rolling by me, they are rockin' easily,
I am older than I once was and younger than I'll be,
That's not unusual. No it isn't strange,
After changes upon changes, we are more or less the same.
After changes, we are more or less the same.'

"Paul Simon has articulated more in a few lines than I did in a 300-page book. If I live to be a hundred, I'm never going to write anything that good."

"How do you know how Paul Simon feels about what he has written?" Elena asked. "For all we know, he has a dark three a.m. of the soul as well. Remember, he also wrote,"

'And a song I was writing is left undone,
I don't know why I spend my time,
Writing songs I can't believe,
With words that tear and strain to rhyme.'

"Well, he does have adoring fans, piles of money, and more awards than he can count," Kathy said.

Ah," replied Elena, "maybe he's using the wrong yardstick too."
The eight of us stopped at the water fountain then walked over to look out over the bay. Elena mentioned Robin Williams--brilliant, talented, successful, adored.

225

And dead by his own hand.

Could his gauge have been imperfect as well?

A number of us in the running group make our livelihoods and our lives creatively. We play music or make art; we create books, write grants, invent ideas. We are authors and professors, artists and editors.

We would do well to feel good about our accomplishments for ourselves independent of how many books we sell or where we finish in our age group in a running event.

The number of Americans who have run sub 2:10 marathons is 12. The number of Kenyans who have run sub 2:10 marathons is 37.

In October.

In 2012, a Kenyan who ran a sub 2:04 marathon didn't even make the Olympic team for his country.

Keep in mind that a 2:10--never mind 2:04--marathon is running a quarter mile in 75 seconds. Then running another quarter miles in 75 seconds.
Then running 103 more quarter miles at 75 seconds.

No one you know has ever run more than a few consecutive 75-second quarter miles. It is entirely likely that no one you currently know could run **one** quarter mile in 75 seconds never mind 105 of them.

Stated another way, you could take a taxicab to the 26th mile marker of a major marathon, jump out and join the race, and still lose.

Badly.

226

Trying to be the best that someone else can be is a stupid criterion for attaining a shot at happiness and positive self-regard.

So why in the name of everything that is good and decent in the world are you forcing this horrific nonsense--that happiness comes with accomplishment--on your beloved children? If Kathy doesn't feel good about having published three books, do you think she would feel better about having written four? If having finished ten marathons doesn't give her a sense of accomplishment and contentment, do you think she would feel better about having run 11? How about 20? How about 100?

Wouldn't it make infinitely more sense to allow your children to be who they are, make their own way, find their own meaning? Don't you think that they're more likely to feel good about themselves from just doing the best they can, making a contribution, being who they are? Wouldn't you like them to feel good about themselves even if they never run a sub 2:10 marathon?

Isn't feeling good about giving it their best shot a better--and more likely--objective?

To hear Kathy beat herself up because she isn't as brilliant, wealthy, and famous as Paul Simon is shameful. Let's all try to help our kids accept themselves for who they are, not for what they can do. Harvard University rather than North Cornstalk College, five novels rather than three, 20 marathons rather than 10, a 2:10 marathon rather than a 4:10.

Having done the best you can rather than doing the best of anybody is a first step in avoiding the madness.

Because the list of what your kids are not going to be the best at is as long as life is short.

63

2 Good 2 Be True

If something sounds too good to be true, that's probably because it's selling some bogus educational product to your children.

Just this morning I got a call from a thoroughly breathless woman who assured me that all the students who take her company's test prep class improve their SAT scores by 350 points. "Imagine that!" I thought. "Several hours of instruction replacing years of development." While she was excitingly blathering on about the excellence of her curriculum and the professionalism of her instructors, I reflected on a conversation I had with a new acquaintance in the gym the other day. "This weight lifting stuff doesn't work," he began. "I've been here every day for a week and I'm still 60 pounds overweight."

There may have been one child somewhere whose score improved from the 50th to the 84thpercentile after short-term intervention. Heck, for all I know, there may be somebody who lost 60 pounds after seven days of working out. One hears about shepherds more often than one meets a man wearing a tunic and holding a crook. I'm going to go out on a limb here and suggest that short term intervention for prodigious score improvements is as unlikely as "Rub this cream between your thighs! Lose weight while you sleep!" and "Play music to your baby in utero!"

Neither of which bogus claim is supported by a scintilla of evidence.

Speaking of shepherds, you know that expression about Rome not being built in a day? Neither was a healthy relationship with a child. I get it. You have to work. It is brutally expensive to live in this town. And there is a lot to be said for living indoors. But at some point you have to make a decision. You are the adult after all. You're going to have to get off the computer at night and hang out with your child. And the younger they are, the easier they are to cuddle up with on the couch.

If you can't take the children camping on a daily basis, how about dedicating an hour a day to sitting on the couch-no electronics for goodness sake!-and just hanging out? What should you talk about? Maybe nothing. Nothing is a good topic. No electronics, no questions, no agenda, no nothing. Because "how was your day?" can be just as intrusive as "What did you get on your math test?" Oh, and while we're on the subject of your child's math test, here's an idea: let it go. Your child knows your opinion of how you feel she should do on her math test. I promise. In almost 40 years of professional practice, I have yet to meet a student who exclaimed doe-eyed to her mom, "You wanted me to do WELL on my math test? That explains everything!"

Trust me on this one: your kid knows how you feel. Keeping your anxiety--eh, ahem, of course, I meant your *opinion*--about her performance to yourself will allow her to be honest about coming to you with the important stuff. Being quiet about what doesn't matter in the long run will allow her to talk to you about what does matter.

One example of which is where babies come from. (Hint: "New Jersey" is not the answer to "Where do babies come from?" Yes, some babies come from New Jersey; no, that's not what she means.)

In short, keep quiet when you can. Then, when your beloved kiddo DOES have something to say--an important discussion about reproductive biology or ethics or how to do the right thing in a complex world--she'll know where to find you. Right there on the couch where you've always been ever since she was little.

Otherwise your parenting plan is equivalent to just "selling" a crummy relationship product. You can blather on all you want about how much you love your kid. But just like I know that the woman promising absurd score improvements is pushing hokum, your child will know that you are more connected to her performance on a math test than you are to the unmitigated joy of just hanging out with her on the couch talking about nothing.

Because anyone who tells you that you can have a good relationship with your child in "just five minutes a day!" might as well be selling weight loss cream or 350 point score improvements.

64

Lesson Learned

My buddy, Sam, a World War II vet and a self-educated lawyer, may not have been the greatest example of what has been called the greatest generation but he would do. When his wife developed health concerns, he did not waver in his devotion. Widowed with three young children, he never complained or faltered. He started out tough and got tougher.

Not that I am recommending growing up on the streets of The Bronx in the depression. To the day he died, Sam carried scars of what he termed "disagreements" he and his buddies had had with groups of kids from adjoining neighborhoods. Asked about his experiences overseas in Northern France in 1943, he would admit, "Yes, the accommodations and the food left something to be desired."

I was friends with Sam's daughters growing up and would see him for holiday get-togethers. Sam would listen with polite incredulity when I would share biographies of the kids two generations removed from his. "So, the 11-year-old burned down his parents' garage," he would say rubbing his chin as if in thought. "I bet he got a big time out for that."

We also discussed Ethan Couch--our knowledge of which was limited to what we read. Even Sam's sense of snark was strained when we looked at the CNN website two years ago:

"... Hollie Boyles, and daughter, Shelby, left their home to help Breanna Mitchell, whose SUV had broken down. Brian Jennings, a youth pastor, was driving past and also stopped to help.

All four were killed when [Ethan Couch's] pickup plowed into the pedestrians..."

Rather than going to jail, Ethan was "sentenced" to what Sam might have termed, "Lindsay Lohan Rehab." A judge described as "lenient" and a defense of "affluenza," got Ethan probation in a facility with a Jacuzzi rather than 20 years in jail.

Sam suggested that we all would have been better served had Ethan been incarcerated. "His blood alcohol level was .24; completely schnockered is .08. Kids like this are never rehabilitated."

It would be easy to agree; it would be easy to have a sense of outrage and loss--one of the people whom Ethan killed had stopped to help the unknown owner of a stopped car.

I am not an expert on incarceration and recidivism. But I am supposed to know something about parenting. How did Ethan come to feel he could brazenly steal beer from Wal-Mart and commit other crimes with impunity?

Sam argued that Ethan had never experienced the consequences for his stupid choices. "Every time he got arrested previously, his parents bought his way out of it.

So let's work our way backward to a simpler "crime and punishment" scenario, one that may be more relevant for my readers: Your middle school child misses a test. It doesn't matter why. She didn't study, she slept in, she forgot, or she got kidnapped by aliens. All loving parents want to intervene with the teacher: "May she take the test tomorrow?" Or worse, a lie: "She had an appointment with the dentist; it wasn't her fault."

My gentle advice is to be sympathetic with your daughter, to listen to her concerns about how horrible it will be to get a zero. And then to let her learn from her mistake. Not because you want to see her punished, but because you want to communicate that she is in control of her own destiny.

A small consequence now can avoid a bigger one later. I have to believe that Ethan's parents rescued, enabled, and softened every possible life lesson that might have come his way. Or as Sam might have remarked about the girl who messed up and missed the test, "She got a bad grade, learned a lesson, and never made the same mistake again? Imagine that."

65

WNEL

A buddy of mine is extraordinary successful. He lectures for a living, has appeared on *Good Morning America*, CNN and countless other national media outlets. He has published more books than I've had hot meals and still finds time to run his training miles every week.

Alan joins our running group whenever he's in town, so it will come as no surprise that I reached out to him for advice on how to market my new book, a copy of which you are now holding. The previous title--<u>Love the Kid you Get. Get the Kid You Love</u>--had sold dozens of copies and I was hoping to hit three-digit sales for my new tome. No one knows more about branding, marketing, and self-promoting books than Alan.

To his credit--we've been friends for over half a century after all--he immediately reached out to contacts and arranged for me to be interviewed on WNEL. He even insisted on driving me to the station. "It's not that easy to get on TV the first time," he cautioned.

Given Alan's success in national media markets, you can imagine my surprise when we pulled up to a small building in a seedy part of town. I saw weeds growing out of cracks in the asphalt in the unkempt parking lot. Passing the entrance door covered with iron burglar bars, I saw mold on the ceiling and a dead plant in the lobby. The sound engineer, who clearly doubled as the bouncer, told us to wait on chairs that were already old and stained when *The Honeymooners* premiered.

"Welcome to WNEL," Alan said as we gingerly sat down.

You've never heard of WNEL, gentle reader? That's okay. Neither has anyone else. WNEL is what Alan calls "W Nobody Ever Listens."

That said, I thought my on-air conversation went pretty well. I talked about college admissions, kids with learning differences, process addictions, and good parenting. The interviewer let me direct the dialog: it was clear to me that he was thinking about his next guest--an attractive 30-something who ran an automotive supply shop--more than he was focused on my insights into how to raise healthy kids in an unhealthy world. In short, I said what I had to say.

But no one was listening--not even the person doing the interview. When I was through with my 15 minutes of--and I use the term loosely--"fame," Alan was engrossed in dictating notes for his next book, his 20th, I believe. Even my buddy who had set up the gig and driven me there hadn't listened.

"How did it go?" he asked.

"Pretty well, I think," I responded. "But I don't think anyone was listening.

"Probably not," Alan agreed. "You have a face for radio."

Given that Alan had been partially responsible for two of my greatest joys in life--he introduced me to both ultra-marathon running and collecting comic books--I left the snarky remark alone. But I did ask him why he drove me across town to an interview on a station that no one would hear. I saw it as a gig that would not benefit me in any foreseeable way. No one listening to that show was going to buy a book on parenting; no one listening to that show was going to become a client; indeed, no one was listening to that show at all.

"What gives?" I asked.

"The first time you do the Oprah Winfrey Show should not be the first time you do a TV interview," he said. "It should be your 100th time."

Ah.

Similarly, the first time you have a conversation with your child about reproductive biology should not be the first time you have a conversation with your child. Having a hundred little conversations with your kids about nothing important lays the groundwork for the big conversation down the road about something critical.

How do we inspire our beloved children to look forward to our interactions? By asking open-ended questions and LISTENING to-- rather than judging--their responses. Whether your response to, "I got a 90 on a math test" is a supportive, "You got a 90, that's so great!" or a derisive, "You got a 90? Don't they give 100s at your school?" you are taking responsibility for your child's feelings. Why not allow for reflection? Refrain from being a hijacker?

"How about that?" or "What do you think?" are value-neutral responses more likely to engender introspection and growth. Children are much more likely to be responsive if they feel they are valued rather than corrected or interrogated.

And besides, the more answers they give to open ended questions, the more likely they are to be well prepared for their interviews--on WNEL or the Oprah Winfrey Show.

66

Attitude of Gratitude

Competent, ethical college admissions counselors wear any number of hats including but not limited to the following:

Coach Chapeau: "C'mon, you! Three more essays! You can DO this! Let's go!"

Mortician Millinery: "I'm sorry your dream of attending North Cornstalk State has passed away..."

Balloon Popper Bowler: "No, that your mother's cousin's ex-wife's neighbor's father-in-law is an alum of Highly Selective College does not improve your chances of admission."

Life Saver Sombrero: "You hate math and got a C in algebra as a senior but are only applying to MIT, Cal Tech, and Worchester Polytechnic Institute; could we talk a little more about your passion for literature and some other schools?"

And of course, Erudite Editor, Proof Reader Extraordinaire.

Chatting recently with Anna about her brilliant, insightful, thoughtful admissions essay, I suggested she consider replacing a coordinating conjunction in the third paragraph with a semicolon.

"A semicolon!" she replied rapturously. "What a great idea!"

Mrs. Riter, Anna's mom, chimed in. "A semicolon fits perfectly! Thank you so much!"

Had I taken a bullet for you in wartime then donated all my organs to your daughter, you could not have been as gracious and grateful as Anna and her mom.

In another office across town, a colleague is trying to untangle the twisted logic and fragment sentences of an applicant's hastily scrawled, hand-written paragraph. "There are some good ideas here," the counselor begins cautiously, "but I wonder if this draft represents your best work."

The child, suffering from a particularly acute bout of affluenza and entitle-isis responds snarkily: "I wanted these applications submitted last week."

240

His mother jumps on. "We paid you a lot of money. I thought you were going to help us with the essays."

The counselor doesn't know where to begin to respond. "It is unethical to write essays for applicants." "Your son will be taking English composition in college next year; it is important that he have some skills." "It is against every ethical tenant of my profession to write rather than edit." Before the counselor can formulate an appropriate answer, the mom summarily fires him, takes her son, and leaves-presumably to buy admissions essays from a slimy counselor elsewhere.

How do loving parents engender an "attitude of gratitude" rather than the insolence of "Buy me; get me; I want it now"? How do we encourage our kids to exude appreciation over a semi-colon rather than whimper about ethical guidance?

Note than complaints are loudest from those who are least likely to benefit from answers and insights.

"Can I buy a house in your neighborhood for $40,00?"

"No," replies the knowledgeable realtor. "Homes here go for an average of $700,000."

"Then you are an incompetent professional, I hate you, and I will devote my life to trashing your reputation," replies the disappointed would-be buyer.

That there are differences between students applying to college is an observation that I am hardly the first to point out. WHY these two children are so spectacularly disparate is worth considering. Yes, their skills are different: the good writer is grateful; the poor applicant is grouchy and unrealistic.

"From an apple tree, you don't get pears." Do grateful parents bring up grateful children? Are skillful children more likely to be appreciative? Or are there other factors at play? Are there examples of children with modest skills who are grateful for help? Are there brilliant, motivated children who not appreciative?

I would be interested in hearing your thoughts.

Before I go back to editing admissions essays.

Best Game

When you are scheduled to meet a client, you take a shower and make sure your shirt is ironed. When both you and the client speak at once, you make sure you are the one to say, "I beg your pardon; go ahead" or "I'm sorry to interrupt. What were you saying?"

You're not being manipulative. It's just common politeness. Under no circumstances would you insult a potential client's political beliefs. You would not presume to suggest that his views on religion might be mistaken.

When you were dating, you were thoughtful and pleasant. You considered how to make a good impression. You were solicitous: "Would you like to go out for Italian or stay home and order in some Chinese?" You even kept your mouth shut about your in-laws.

Benjamin Franklin's admonished us, "Keep your eyes wide open before marriage, half shut afterwards." Which brings us to today's question: Are you bringing your best game to your kids?

Or are you sitting on the metaphorical couch, insisting that your kids straighten up and fly right when you, to the contrary, are slouched and scratching? Are you requiring that the kids be respectful when you are sarcastic?

Don't misunderstand. I get it. I know how hard you work and how little time you have for nonsense once you get home. No one is more entitled than you given what you put up with during the week. Yes, your boss is an idiot; no, your unpaid overtime isn't appreciated; yes, you deserve some peace and quiet on the weekend so you can just kick back and watch the ballgame.

So, of course you can have a glass of wine with dinner. Who would presume to deny you that modest pleasure? But look at it from your kid's point of view: What if your child needs to be back at school in the evening for play practice? If you've had a third glass of wine, your kid misses fulfilling her commitment to her fellow cast members or is concerned about being driven by an impaired parent. Both bad alternatives could have been obviated by waiting for the weekend to open that bottle.

A distinction must be drawn between what is in your child's interest and what you are justifying with your own imperfect and maybe irrational beliefs. "Spare the rod and spoil the child" is now accepted

244

as abuse. Under what circumstances could it ever have been okay to hit your kid?

Frank McCourt's 1996 <u>Angela's Ashes</u> recounts a dad who seldom works and drinks his paycheck rather than buy bread and milk for his starving children when he does find jobs. Before I break my arm patting myself on the back telling myself that I'm certainly doing a better job than that drunk, let me think critically about what I'm giving my children and what I'm depriving them of.

I bring my best game to work or I lose my job; I bring my best game to the world of dating or I don't find connection and intimacy; but if I don't bring my best self to my sacred obligation to be the best parent that I can be, then the consequences of my inadequate performance aren't felt for some time.

Making the hard choices isn't about being weak or giving in to the demands of tiny terrorists. It's easy to say, "Go ahead and play on your iPad" rather than "give me a hand with bathing the dog." It's gutless to say, "sure, you can watch a third hour of the Disney Channel" instead of "cuddle up here with me on the couch and I'll read you chapter nine of <u>Winnie the Pooh</u>"

But you can't have it both ways. Either bring up the kid yourself or accept the fact that some other values are going to be the pervading ones. The children's television channels seem to be doing an adequate job of promoting snarkiness as a fundamental value. But I never met a kid who would prefer to watch crappy television rather than go on a hike with family and friends.

Your kids don't need perfect parents, but they need good enough parents. Let's all commit to doing the best job we can with our most important responsibility.

68

The Child You Want

A buddy of mine turned 50 the other day. On an early morning run, he whined yet again about how he hasn't met anyone who meets his criteria for an amorous association.

"Of course she should be bright and funny, but she should also be physically attractive and enjoy old horror movies, right?"

A group of runners sped up and a few others slowed down. We had all heard these criteria explicated so many times over the years we could recite them ourselves. Many of our group of a dozen sweaty folks work hard on our relationships and our families. Nobody wants to hear from guy who has never been married and probably never will be.

"And I don't want anybody over 30 years old," he went on. "And nobody who wants to have children. You know I don't like kids. And she has to be sensitive to my schedule. You know I work nights, so she has to be available to hang out after 10:00 pm and understand that I like to sleep on the weekends. And she should have her own money and be generous because I don't make that much." Without irony or insight, he continued, "Is that too much to ask?"

We all enjoy Jim. But after 30 years, nobody takes him seriously. What he wants in a girlfriend is as unrealistic as it is unreasonable. His salary from managing a small restaurant doesn't make him an economic catch--not that he's all that bighearted to begin with. The likelihood of his connecting with a physically attractive, financially independent, 30-something who wants to hang out with a demanding man 20 years her senior is zero. He wants to find somebody who wants to watch TV reruns late at night? Horror movies? C'mon. Not gonna happen.

There are many ways to find someone with whom you want to spend romantic time. One critical strategy is to widen the net so that there is some possibility that a fish might be caught. Unless Jim makes some fundamental changes in his criteria or in himself, he is going to be watching late night TV alone.

Now admittedly, I don't know much about dating, but I have given some thought over the years to how parents interact with their children. Here's an analogous question regarding accepting your kids for who they are: Is it possible that you are insisting that your child be only one kind of child? Are you like Jim who is looking for only one kind of partner? Will you only be satisfied with one kind of child?

If your vision of who your child should be extends only to a high achieving, academic superstar who is athletically gifted and editor of the high school yearbook, the likelihood is that you will be disappointed. By definition, only one child can have the highest grades at a particular school. Can you live with the fact that your child may not be the valedictorian? Only one student can be the editor of the yearbook. Are you okay with the possibility that the editor could be somebody else's kid?

I would never be the one to say that otherwise your dissatisfaction is inevitable. Nor would I presume to suggest that you might want to look at your own issues. But I might ask why is it so important to you that your child be who you want her to be--valedictorian, athlete, editor--rather than who she wants herself to be.

Was the model in your family of origin displeasure and frustration? Were your parents typically irritated and disapproving rather than loving and supportive? Was their love contingent upon your performance rather than forthcoming regardless of how you did?

If you accept your kids for who they are rather than for how they do, there is a better chance that you will have the kind of relationship that you want--close, communicative, and connected. If, on the other hand, you are only accepting of one kind of kid, let me introduce you to my friend, Jim. You two may have a lot to talk about and a great deal of time in which to do so.

69

Ethical Admissions

"How has the college admissions process changed in the 30-something years that I have been helping students choose and apply to college?"

When I give talks or appear on radio shows, I typically point out how students are filling in more applications and that therefore it's harder to predict who will be admitted where. I talk about "yield"--

the number of admitted students who actually matriculate. If Tommy applies to 14 colleges and is offered a spot at eight of them, there are seven schools where he doesn't show up. It's increasingly hard for those seven schools to make good predictions about the size of their first year classes.

The Common Application has its pluses, but allowing colleges to know who is likely to be on campus the following fall is not one of them. A generation ago, filling in an application by hand or with a typewriter was a commitment. Remember trying to line up your answers to "name," "address," and "phone number" on your portable selectric? Remember white out? Remember tearing up the mangled application and getting up the courage to write to the college to request another copy?

But the biggest change since I started advising families in 1983 is that parents no longer even pretend to be subtle about their perception of college admissions as an arms race. "Duke or Die!" is ingrained in both generations. Perhaps, as a result of the stress, parents don't even pretend to model ethical behavior in the admissions process.

Frankie, a good student, mentions that he was the treasurer of the Future Business Leaders of America Club at his private school.

"Write down that you were president," his unblinking mother says.

"But I wasn't president, mom," Frankie replies.

His mom continues: "How would they know?"

Of course, I found the above conversation horrifying. Poor Frankie, who now has to contradict his mother in order to fill in an accurate application. And poor Frankie's mom. What a burden it must be to believe that unless your child is admitted to Duke that his life will be lessened in some way. Imagine teaching your child that it's okay to lie.

I gently explained that independent counselors cannot be part of a process that involves falsifying applications. Frankie's mom just looked at me. Maybe she was waiting for me to wink and say, "Just kidding." Maybe she thought I would ask her for more money. I can think of many meetings over the years that I have enjoyed more.

The good news is that there is a big win for families who are willing to go about the process of filling in applications in an appropriate way.

If you refuse to encourage your children to exaggerate, prevaricate, and fib on their applications, there is less likelihood that they will grow up to be criminal psychopaths arrested and imprisoned for stealing pension funds.

Kohlberg taught us about the stages of moral development. A young child might not steal a cookie for fear of getting caught. An older child might not steal a cookie considering that there might not be enough cookies for everyone. I would argue that Frankie's mom clearly wants all the cookies for herself.

Kids learn what they live. Model joy, acceptance. "Don't do things. Be things." Communicate that your kids will be okay if they go to Duke or some "lesser" school. Let your kids know that you believe in them because they have your good values and morals.

Kids who get screamed at learn how to get screamed at or how to scream. Abused kids learn how to be abused or how to abuse. And kids who are taught to lie learn how to lie. On the other hand, kids who are respected learn how to be respectful.

How do loving parents bring up healthy kids in a world overrun with people like Frankie's mom? Communicate to your kids at every

251

opportunity: I love you for who you are, not for what you do. You are my beloved child whether you are admitted to this college or that. And in our family, behaving honorably is more important than being president of the Future Business Leaders of America.

70

Shh, I'm Hunting Wabbits

Scholars disagree about the number of books in the Library at Alexandria when it was destroyed some 2300 years ago last Thursday. Estimates range from 40,000 to 400,000 volumes. Even using the larger guess, an approximation of the sum total of accrued information available to the most learned academicians of antiquity is equivalent to the number of bytes contained in a video depicting a man inadvertently falling off the end of a dock into a lake.

To have access to the sum total of human knowledge of philosophy, literature, and mathematics, travelling through the Egyptian desert is no longer necessary. A few mouse clicks will suffice. As Wikipedia founder Jimmy Wales says, "Imagine a world in which every single person on the planet is given free access to the sum of all human knowledge. That's what we're doing."

And that's a good thing. But galumphing down the information highway has an unintended and heartrending consequence: no more absurd arguments, no more bar fights.

Everybody knows that the Yankees have appeared in and won more World Series games than any other team in the history of the MLB. But who is in second place in October appearances?

Before we all came to rely on Wikipedia, I would have said Dodgers; you might have said Pirates, and we could have had an engaging evening spouting vociferously:

"The Dodgers beat the Milwaukee Braves in seven games in 1959!"

"No, they didn't, you nimrod," you could respond. That was 1958 and they LOST to the Braves!"

The conversation could degenerate gloriously from there with spirited cries of "Braves are terrible!" and "The Dodgers leaving Brooklyn heralded the end of civilization!"

Subsequently, we could "settle things" by shoving one another in an alley or threatening to tell one another's parents how the dent in the door of their 1967 Dodge Dart actually got there. Good times.

And the brawl need not end at closing time. I knew guys in college who have been arguing for generations about the 1908 Cubs or whether Anne Boleyn was the one who died or was divorced.

254

Consider an even more glorious situation from the following lyric:

I hit him hard right between the eyes
And he went down, but to my surprise,
He come up with a knife and cut off a piece of my ear.
So I busted a chair right across his teeth
And we crashed through the wall and into the street
Kicking and a gouging in the mud and the blood and the beer.

In 2016, a quick Internet search will determine a potential ancestor's location; a paternity test is inexpensive and accurate. There is no need to go to Gatlinburg in mid-July.

A few clicks will identity of the team with the second most World Series wins (St. Louis, as it happens.) And that Anne Boleyn was executed. Tragic really. The death of that nice woman and the fact that all arguments can be settled without threats of physical harm.

The point is that accessing information is no longer an issue for our children. Being inundated and overwhelmed with information is.

Your children don't need more stimulus; they need less. Your children need quiet, they need time for reflection, they need someone--preferably everyone--to hush up for an hour or two so that they can think, reflect, and regroup. In the library at Alexandria, your kids could choose what book to read; today they are unprotected from what they don't want exactly when they don't need it.

Everyone reading my book has been exposed to salespeople who never shut up and are, therefore, ineffectual. We have been harangued by telemarketers who are trained not to allow us to interrupt long enough to say, "Please delete me from this calling list." Job applicants who talk about themselves incessantly never get

hired. The four most important words of sales are "Shut the f***
up!"

And dating? Don't get me started. Nobody wants to go out with the
person who spends the entire evening blathering incessantly about
accomplishments large and small: "And then after successfully
completing the merger and acquisition, I went skiing in Switzerland
and could I have that dressing on the side?"

Check, please.

So let's divide out communication with our kids into two distinct
groups, those messages that are about us as opposed to those that
allow the kids to be heard. In the first group, in which the parent is
the one speaking, a tremendous flood of information washes over
the kid: "Don't forget to put your cleats in the car because after you
finish your math homework, we're going to swing by your
grandmother's house to drop off the lasagna." Nothing wrong with
soccer, algebra, or mozzarella, but what a lot of words for many
fourth graders.

Open-ended questions offer kids the opportunity to reflect. As does
silence. Surely there can be one hour, maybe even ALL the hours
after 8:00 at night, when there is an end to texting, Google, Internet,
and email. Imagine a home in which everyone-that means you too,
mom-puts the electronics aside.

In The Right Stuff, Tom Wolfe writes cogently about a trained
fighter pilot who is so overwhelmed with stimulus-he is talking on
the radio, firing machine guns, taking evasive action, and trying to
keep himself and his crew from being blown to bits after all-that he
doesn't hear his co-pilot screaming that there are incoming missiles.
Is it possible that your kids are similarly stunned with information
and that is why they forget to take the trash buckets to the street on
Mondays and Thursdays?

256

The Buddha teaches, "Wait for the question." Shouldn't we allow our children the peace and quiet and the psychic space to come up with a query or two.

Teachable Decade

Dumb questions used to make me want to climb up a tower and hurl dry erase markers at random folks walking below. "I. Just. Went. Over. That." I would sputter through clenched teeth. "Cosecant is the reciprocal of sine; cosecant is not a punk rock group."

Remember the man teaching the horse to eat less and less? Just before he has convinced the poor brute to eat only a few strands of hay each day, the emaciated animal dies. Similarly, I congratulated myself on eliminating questions. My classroom was quiet. Silence is golden.

Of course what I hadn't eliminated was any imperfections in my students' understanding of trigonometry. My anger had forced them to be quiet, not to comprehend. My impatience had forced them to favor cheating over love of subject matter. My sarcastic putdowns had engendered an atmosphere of fear not a classroom with mutual support.

As a more mature teacher I came to appreciate that if kids aren't asking questions, it's not because they know the material. If kids aren't making mistakes, it's because they're disconnected and lost. If students aren't asking dumb questions, it's because they've given up. Just as pain in the body's way of communicating that you might want to move your hand away from the fire, questions are a way of taking the intellectual temperature of a group of learners. $\text{Sin}^2 x = 1 - \cos^2 x$ just as surely as no questions equals no understanding.

If students already know how to graph $y = 2 \tan x$ then I'm unemployed. Seriously. What good am I blathering on in front of all those high school kids if they already know how to graph all the trig functions? I can be replaced by a curriculum on a computer. And maybe I deserve to be.

Students who don't know trig means jobs for trig teachers. Children who don't know that starting a science project at nine o'clock the night before it's due when the stores are closed and no, we don't just happen to have a two-foot by three-foot piece of poster board lying around, why do you ask? equals jobs for parents.

The typical response, "How many times do I have to tell you to write down your assignments in your calendar? Now I'm going to have to stay up half the night helping you with this stupid project. Don't you ever listen to me?" is unlikely to engender honest communication subsequently. Nor is your child going to learn anything positive from the experience of being berated. Chances are she already feels overwhelmed with bad feelings about not having started on the project three weeks ago when it was assigned. She may need support; she may need help with her electronic calendar. She does not need to be harangued and humiliated.

You might THINK your fantasy is living with a movie star in a mansion being waited on by smiling servants telling you that your polo pony is saddled. In reality you are much happier with the life you have. You THINK you want the child who has already done her homework and doesn't need any guidance, advice, correction or occasional emotional interchange. In actuality, every mistake your child makes is an opportunity for you to gently instruct and share your values. In short, a chance to teach.

If your kids aren't making mistakes, you're unemployed. As a parent, you're useless. And believe me, if your kids aren't getting their values from you, they are most certainly absorbing standards and beliefs elsewhere.
Next time your kid messes up (chances are by the time you finish reading this paragraph) try to keep these two thoughts in mind:

1) Nobody ever learned anything by being yelled at.

2) Now is my chance to get in the game and do some good.

If I learned to refrain from going thermonuclear when a 16-year-old didn't know her trigonometric identities, surely your can avoid going apoplectic when your kids need you the most.

I'll stop writing now so you and your eighth grader can sit down and work calmly on organizing her assignment pad.

260

72

War Games

Before Matthew Broderick was Ferris Beuller and Ally Sheedy was the weird girl in "Breakfast Club," the kids starred in "War Games," an uplifting film about global thermonuclear war and the end of all life on the planet, that sort of thing. Spoiler alert: the world does not come to a fiery end in the final reel. An out of control computer runs simulations--hence the "game" in the film's title--all of which end in the planet more or less being blown to bits no bigger than your lawn furniture. Our heroes, Matt and Ally are able to "teach" the machine that the only way to win the game is not to play. The War Operation Plan Response learns that no strategic placement of jet fighters or aircraft carriers will lead to one side "winning" a nuclear conflagration. Ultimately the WOPR is able to squawk in its distended computer voice, "How about a nice game of chess?" as we stand down from Defcom Five and our empty popcorn containers hit the trash buckets.

If a computer with an unfortunate acronym (WOPR. Really?) can determine that thermonuclear war is not winnable, can loving parents of high school students come to a similarly virtuous conclusion? Here are the numbers. Not the arithmetic regarding how many Soviet nuclear submarines float off the coast of Vladivostok, but the most recent stats regarding how many kids get admission offers at selected selective schools.

Seventy years ago when Warren Buffet was rejected at Harvard (big "oops," dontcha think?), the school admitted 245 out of 278 applicants from prestigious prep schools, a whopping 88%. Fast forward to the past five years: Harvard's overall admit rate has been 6.9%, 5.8%, 5.9%, 5.3%, and 5.1%. We're talking one yes for every 15 nopes.

I have written elsewhere and endlessly about the arbitrariness of selective admissions. I have pontificated in these chapters about how hard it is to predict who will be the one yep out of the stack of 15 "we wish you every success elsewhere." I have reminded my readers that valedictorian applicants with 1600 SATs who speak five languages, have patented inventions, and built nuclear submarines in their basements are routinely rejected. Today I want to help you understand how completely and utterly worthless is the whole silly process.

Because becoming that valedictorian with the 1600 SATs and patented inventions who walks on water and pees perfume can cost a kid, if not her immortal soul, then certainly her childhood. With less "perfect" credentials the odds drop off from one in 16 to significantly less. At "only" top five percent, the odds are closer to one in 50. If a kid "achieves" that academic pinnacle--first in her class--her odds at Stanford, Columbia or Princeton are still single digits. Who needs this?

Valedictorians are smart nowadays, no argument. But they also put in endless hours carrying buckets of knowledge back and forth. They learn some stuff that excites them and has meaning, but they do a ton of work that is insipid and quickly forgotten. "Top" kids are motivated, but they are also stressed and, if I may speak frankly, frequently frazzled to the point of being unpleasant to be around. There is something ungracious about the unending competition and recomputing of grade point averages.

So here's some non non-directed advice for high school students concerned about their applications to college (read: every high school student): take the AP courses that are of interest. Don't take every AP course offered just to take a shot at being graduated at the very top of your class. Develop passion and commitment outside the classroom, not a compendium of insipid community service hours. Become involved in activities that have meaning for you whether or not you think those undertakings will "look good" at Dartmouth or Rice. Read a book that isn't assigned for goodness sake. Take some time off. Go for a hike with friends. Make a minor mistake and deal with the consequences. In short, have a life. The WOPR is a machine; you, to the contrary, are a person. There's a difference.

Here's some non non-directed advice for parents of high school students: focus on your child, not on admissions. If your child loves reading, if your child loves learning, if your child is motivated, if your child is content, the future will take care of itself. Still concerned about college? I promise you that there are hundreds of colleges that accept virtually every qualified applicant and that the kids who do well at those institutions get admitted to medical school just the same as the kids who went to the single digit admit schools.

Because the only way to win is not to play.

73

Opportunity

"What if the impressionists had been dentists?" queried a droll essay in 1978. A more intriguing question considers what might have ensued had Wayne Gretsky been born in South Miami.

In baseball, pundits argue about the greatest player of all time. Ted Williams or Willie Mays. Barflies pontificate about Walter Payton versus Johnny Unitas as the best football player ever. In every sport, there is room for glorious debate. Except hockey. Wayne Gretsky is far and away the best ever to dodge a Zamboni. Even without his all-time record goals, he would still have more points than anyone who ever played the game. Nothing to talk about.

But what if Wayne's family had lived down the street from me here in South Miami where the nearest ice skating rink is a three-day trek away by wagon train over rocky terrain? Or worse, what if Wayne's parents had forbidden him to play hockey insisting instead that he study linguistics?

What if loving parents are searching in the wrong haystack? Insisting that your kids suffer with piano lessons when they could be brilliant programmers is ill advised. So is demanding that your kids learn Chinese when they could be gifted mathematicians. Forcing your children to study calculus when they could be fulfilled as musicians always turns out badly.

Imagine Wayne Gretsky growing up to be the manager of the Winn-Dixie down the block because he never got the chance to strap on ice skates. Think of the lost opportunities for your children to achieve greatness and contentment by following their own star. Shouldn't they be exposed to every opportunity? Shouldn't they be allowed to find their own path?

Which is not to say that any of the above choices are mutually exclusive. Good academicians can be strong athletes. Gifted musicians can do well in calculus. The question is about the use of excessive *force*.

As an adult, consider an insensitive employer forcing you to complete tasks for which you have neither aptitude nor affinity. Complete the nightmare by envisioning your boss constantly on your case: "Have you finished those reports yet?"

266

Is it any wonder that people hate their jobs and steal office supplies? Workplace misery doesn't *excuse* theft but it might help to *explain* all those missing staplers.

What if you are forcing your children to devote their attention to that which is antithetical to their nature? Sure, I can multiply two-digit numbers together in my head, but does that mean that my children must learn the same party trick? What if we are rubbing our children's metaphorical fur the wrong way?

The smart money is on allowing our children every opportunity to be who they are. <u>Offer</u> them athletics, music, art, academics and every other conceivably option to find their passion and their brilliance. Expose them to skating and literature and language and hiking. <u>Model</u> sober attention to that which brings you joy.

"Love what you do and you'll never work a day in your life." Whatever else we communicate as parents, insisting that our children fulfill <u>our</u> vision of the path that will bring them contentment is invariably a step in the wrong direction.

Or as Gretsky himself said, "You miss all the shots you don't take." Surely we should put as many metaphorical hockey sticks in the hands of our very real children as possible.

The "Idiot-athon"

Of all the gloriously exuberant excesses of the "Idiot-athon", surely
the shuttle run was the silliest and the most fun. After running 10,
20, 30, 40, and 50 yards out picking up and putting down blocks of
wood, competitors were required to remove a plastic bone-the femur
if memory serves-in the game of "Operation." Touching the side
with the tweezers added a 30 second penalty to the run time.
Noteworthy how shaky our hands were after all that sprinting.

Running, biking, and swimming were on the syllabus every year. Canoeing and archery were frequent events. But the remaining five contests varied from bench press to standing broad jump, from running 100 yards with a 75-pound sack of sand on our shoulders to softball throw.

If I stunk at shot put and pull-ups, I could make up points in the endurance events. A Florida boy born and bred, I could handle a canoe pretty well and enjoyed watching stronger competitors boink back and forth while I steered gracefully out and back around the bouy. I placed in the middle of the pack on the obstacle course, fast up the net but slow over the eight-foot wood barriers.

Such a gloriously stupid contest; such fun. A decathlon for the young at heart, a splendid competition with ribbons and fried chicken for all competitors. Who won? Who remembers? Who cares?

The camaraderie and fellowship were also first rate. We all shouted outrageously for one another, giving advice and encouragement. "Watch out for the three-foot drop at mile four of the mountain bike course!" "Don't slip in the mud at the turn around point on the obstacle course!"

A snarkier competitor could argue that cheering, support, and guidance make no sense if anybody actually cared about winning or losing. Somebody gets five points for first place and somebody else doesn't. In a sense, encouraging a competitor is arguing against your own interest. But again, in the glorious South Florida sunshine covered in sand and sweat, who could possibly care who came in first or last? "Play hard; play fair. Nobody hurt."

In selective college admissions on the other hand, many would argue that the stakes are higher. Statistics are readily available regarding regular and early decision. Counselors openly share advice about essay topics: "DON'T write about the death of your kitten!" And everybody knows how to maximize a student's chances of getting in off the waitlist. The advice is simple and straightforward. Bring to the attention of the admissions committee any new information. Write a polite email pointing out improvements in test scores or grades. And tell the college that if admitted to OBU that you will attend.

IF Old Brick University is indeed your first choice.

Which is why I was outraged to learn of a colleague who gave advice to a student who was "waitlisted" at three "top" schools. The counselor advised the student to tell all three colleges "if admitted, I will attend."

Which, obviously, was not true.

This counselor was trying to confer an unfair advantage. She recommended that her student cheat. The line between encouragement--"proofread your essay carefully"--and fraud--telling more than one school you will show up if admitted--is clear.

No new first year beds are invented for the cheater. The freshman class doesn't get bigger by one student. The student only takes the place of some other child. In my estimation, the other child is probably more deserving.

This counselor's inappropriate advice shames ethical advisors everywhere. This inappropriate practice is a long way from men and women splendidly racing through a glorious South Florida morning, trying to keep their hands from shaking as they remove a plastic femur after a sprint.

75

Jefferson on Education

"Educate and inform the whole mass of the people... They are the only sure reliance for the preservation of our liberty.

That's as may be, but the issue of who gets educated where remains unresolved 200 years after Jefferson wrote about our fledgling democracy.

It is not news that those from enriched environments are more likely to get a jump on the prospect of superior venues and results. Kids who grow up with a bath of language have an advantage over those whose baby sitters are glowing rectangles.

One of my colleagues at a competitive day school was my student years ago. She doesn't give me insider information based on our long-standing relationship. Nor does she give preference to students whom I counsel. She does speak to me plainly without the euphemisms and edu-babble that characterize much of the communication between admissions offices and the broader culture.

"If a child from an enriched background doesn't score in the 90th percentile on norm referenced tests, we are hard pressed to offer him a place in the sixth grade class," Nicole has told me over the decades. "We just have too many kids with high scores. We have to make some guesses about who is going to perform."

The disconnect for me is that the headmaster of Nicole's school brags incessantly about the results of their students. "Of the one hundred seniors at Barrister and Thistledown last year, 94 of them took at least one advanced placement course and 52 of them took three of more AP tests. The number of students who earned a passing score (a 3 or above on a scale of 5) numbered over 80%."

The headmaster pauses as if revealing the winning lotto numbers for the drawing next week: "Last year thirty percent of B & T graduates were admitted to ivy league schools" he says, his voice a throaty whisper.

Perhaps the following simple analogy will make my exasperation apparent: Imagine two hospitals, both of which admitted a thousand patients this month. At Hospital A, 179 of those patients died. At Hospital B, 23 people died.

Which is the better hospital?

For those of you who said Hospital A because 179 is a bigger number than 23, I have two questions, only one of which is snarky and rude:

1) Do you think I have so little respect for my gentle readers to ask a questions with such a simple, obvious answer? This is my third book for goodness sake. I am honored to have thousands of good folks graciously consider my musings. Did I attract such a large following by wasting the time of the good folks who are kind enough to consider my thoughts? Certainly not!

2) What if Hospital A works with victims of violence, gun shot wounds, construction accidents, and car crashes while Hospital B does tummy tucks, Botox injections, and boob jobs? Wouldn't you expect a higher mortality rate at the hospital working with the desperately injured, half-dead? If you took those unfortunates with the severed limbs to Hospital B, you can bet more than just 179 of them would die. Without trauma surgeons, reserves of blood products, and the Jaws of Life, those poor folks wouldn't have a snowball's chance.

Hospital A is the better hospital. Unless you have terminal wrinkles on your forehead.

Similarly, bragging about college placement statistics is misleading. Given the best of the best among sixth grade applicants, it is no surprise that those kiddos end up with good scores and admissions to top schools six years later. Of course those kids do well. Why wouldn't they?

"Of the boys thus sent in any one year, trial is to be made at the grammar schools one or two years, and the best genius of the whole selected, and continued six years, and the residue dismissed. By this means twenty of the best geniusses (sic) will be raked from the rubbish annually..."

Thomas Jefferson, the father of democracy, considered picking the number of kids who fit in one classroom today from a population of hundreds of kids. The rest were to be "dismissed." The question today revolves around what to do with those who have been dismissed. Pretending that the "top" schools produce top kids is as absurd as suggesting that Hospital A kills patients. What to do with the vast majority of kids who aren't in the top ten percent remains a question.

If it turns out that your kid is not one of the selected few attending Barrister and Thistledown, then accepting and loving her for who she is rather than beating her up for not being someone else would be a great first step.

274

76

Achievement, Contentment

A loving mother joined our running group a year ago. Alexa only wants what is best for her children, aged three, five, and seven. "My oldest is brilliant and accomplished," she began as we headed out into the early morning mist. "He excels at everything."

The older members of our group nodded in unison like toy bobble heads, remembering years ago when every developmental milestone could be ticked off with grace and assurance. No one had the heart to interrupt Alexa and mention that the road ahead is seldom without bumps or potholes.

"He does well at karate, he does well at baseball, he does well at school, he's reading above grade level," Alexa went on.

The rest of the older runners remained silent, waiting for the other shoe to drop.

"It's just that he never wants to do anything. He does well when he gets to karate or baseball and seems to enjoy school and activities. But it's becoming a struggle to get him out of the house."

"Does he have time alone at home just to hang out or play with his brothers?" Elena asked. "When I look back, I sometimes wonder if my kids would have benefitted from a little more unstructured time."

"We don't want him to fall behind," Alexa countered gently. "All the other kids are involved in activities pretty much every day after school--gymnastics, ballet tutoring. One kid is already playing French horn AND doing archery. We want our son to be exposed to every possibility so that he can shine."

Most of the other runners in our group are older--late 50s rather than mid-30s--and our kids are grown and gone. I think I speak for many of us when I suggest that our influence on our beloved children was significantly less than we thought. But since I'm supposed to know something about how to bring up healthy kids in a tough culture, I spoke up. I asked Alexa what her long-term goals are for her sons.

She responded instantly. "Obviously, I want them to be happy," she began. "But most importantly, I want them to make a contribution. I want them to be somebody."

"Then you may have the order backwards," I said. "Everybody thinks that achievement leads to contentment. Whereas in my experience, it's the other way around."

We stopped running to wait for some early morning cars to pass. Alexa paused then spoke rapidly. "You mean to tell me that a student isn't happy when she is graduated from medical school? An accomplishment like that means the world to the family and to the graduate."

"I mean they're able to climb that pyramid because they're high functioning. It's not being graduated that makes them happy."

"But we don't want him to fall behind," Alexa said. "It's a competitive world out there. And what about the kid down the block who is already on his second year of French horn lessons?"

"I wish him every success," I said. "But it sounds like your son would rather spend a little more time at home, a little less time being driven to structured activities."

"He does seem happiest when he's reading to his two little brothers," Alexa sighed. "He says he wishes he had more time to draw pictures with them. They make up these incredible, complete worlds with drawings of dinosaurs and they're always asking me to help them with the big words. They create these entire books. They're so beautiful. But then we have to get in the car. With three of them, we're always going somewhere."

"Then it might be a good time to think about 'ages and stages'. Or put another way "present mirth hath present laughter,'" Elena said.

"You mean it's okay if they just hang out at the house on the weekends?"

"Maybe even preferable," I said. "After all, your oldest is only seven years old."

Elena went on. "I don't remember taking my kids anywhere besides the park near our house. They seemed to find enough to do making up games to play in the woods and they seemed to have turned out okay."

Our group stopped at the water fountain. Half of us walked through the parking lot at Matheson Hammock to watch the first light come over the Bay. The sun was just coming up over the horizon and we could barely make out the string of islands and the bridges connecting them to the mainland.

I like to think that many of us felt content thinking about the day to come, whether or not there was a French horn waiting for us back at the office. I hope Alexa's kids--half a century from now when they are my age--will be able to enjoy a misty morning running with a group of friends down to the water fountain looking out over the Bay.

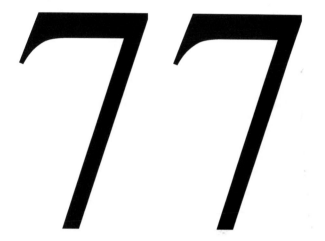

Teacher's Lament

Teachers from across the country appeared to me last night in a dream. With one voice they spoke: "Here's why teachers feel that we can't tell parents the truth about their children."

"Because the parents aren't nice to us never mind respectful. They treat us like coke machines. When they see us at Publix on a Sunday morning, they don't ask us how we're feeling, about the health of our children, or how our parents are getting on. They don't ask us if we're going to watch the Dolphin game later. Instead, they ask us if we've graded the tests yet. And if we have spent the weekend marking papers, they go on to ask us what grade Priscilla got. Then they go on to tell us WHY she got an A or why she didn't get an A. Then they go to talk to us about Priscilla's interactions with her soccer coach and why she didn't score a goal in the game yesterday. Next they remind us about her upcoming sessions with a psychologist for an evaluation because they think she might have some learning differences just like her father's sister. As our eyes glaze over and we feel our legs go numb, they go on to tell us about how her father's sister didn't do well in school and they ask us whether or not there might be a genetic component to Priscilla's learning differences."

"As if we're geneticists. As if we have any idea. As if we have nothing better to do with our Sunday morning than discuss the genealogy of their ex-husband's family."

"That's why we don't tell them the truth: that Priscilla is doing the best she can with the gifts she has; that she's not as smart as her parents think she is or as hard-working as they would like her to be. In short, we're scared to tell them the truth--that Priscilla just isn't going to grow up to teach orthopedic surgery at Harvard Medical School. She doesn't have the horses; she doesn't have the whip. She could be a happy little girl if her parents would stop pressuring her, criticizing her, doing her homework for her, making her feel like she's not okay as she is. But if we tell them the gentle truth--that Priscilla is not likely to win the next Nobel Prize in physics--they explain that it's our fault. If only we would teach better, Priscilla would be getting grades of A+ in AP Calculus. If only we were more sensitive to Priscilla's learning differences, Priscilla would get a Ph.D. in philosophy while pitching the seventh game of the World Series and rule the world."

"Not all of the parents with whom we work are this self-centered, and lacking in simple social graces, but enough are. One is too many. Their boorishness makes it hard to teach because we are constantly concerned about what over-the-top craziness they're going to come up with next."

"We love teaching. Or we did. We wanted to share our passion, our love of our subject, our love of learning, our concern for developing minds. But we are scared to express joy, because the parents misinterpret every misrepresented tidbit of information that comes home."

"And perish forbid we try to gently correct their child. If we suggest that a child read a book the parents undermine our authority and tell us why Percy shouldn't have to read a book, how it wasn't his fault that he didn't read the book, and why should he have to read books anyway?"

"Not only are parents obsessed with their kids to the point of ignoring the most basic social niceties, but the worst of their unbearable diatribe is the outgrowth of their overwhelming anxiety. They don't trust us to do our jobs to the best of our ability. They treat us like hired kitchen help from a lower social class."

"If there were anything the parents could say to change things for the better, teachers would listen. But telling the teachers that our classrooms are underfunded isn't helpful. Are you kidding? The parents think we don't know that our budget for maps, books, magazines, computers, rulers, glue, construction paper, colored pencils, copy paper, and even soap in the bathroom comes from the bake sales rather than from the legislature? Do parents think that we didn't get the memo about how there's no money for anything that we need to teach effectively?"

"We're not in control. We don't have input over the budget. We know what supplies, books, crayons, and manipulatives we'd like to have for the kids to work with. We have even less say about curriculum. We're always being told to teach to some vacuous norm-referenced test. Over two thirds of us are outraged as these inaccurate and insensitive assessments. No one asked us; no one gave us a choice. But parents harangue us about testing as if we woke up one morning and decided tormenting your children was a good idea."

"Because there's one insensitive, boorish parent in each classroom, I am concerned about sharing my passion. That's why I find it hard to teach. Knowing that there are parents who are going to second guess my every professional decision makes me nervous. That's why sensitive teachers are leaving the profession in droves."

"Here's a not so subtle hint: Next time you see me in the grocery store, don't ask me about your child. Don't ask me if I have graded the math tests yet. Don't tell me what I'm doing wrong or how my classroom should be operating more smoothly. Ask me what I think of the weather or if I've read any good books lately. Or ask me how I think the Dolphins are going to do next year."

"Then offer to help out in my classroom."

I woke up at as the amalgam of teachers faded away. I determined to be more attuned to the their needs. I hope my gentle readers will do the same.

78

Night Sacrifice

By the time I met Louise 20 years ago, her children were grown and gone, but I got to know her pretty well toward the end of her life. We agreed that it was tough to grow vegetables in the rocky soil of our neighborhood. We agreed that folks drove too fast down our suburban street. We disagreed about politics so the subject never came up. She wasn't going to change my mind and I wasn't going to shake her convictions. Religion is another topic we judiciously avoided.

Our neighborly conversations about yard work, hurricane preparedness, and mystery novels gave way over the years to biography. My stage of life was clear: car pool, camping trips, getting kids to help with the dishes. Louise, it turned out, had been a stay at home mom for the first few years of her marriage after the war. But her husband got sick, so she went back to school and got a degree in nutrition. She raised three kids, worked at the hospital, and cared for her failing husband for nine years before he died.

I couldn't help but think that her devotion and hard work were extraordinary and I mentioned my impression of the difficult path she had walked. "You made the lunches, got all the kids to school, cleaned the house, worked full time, cared for your ailing husband? That's really something. Nowadays, people LEAVE their families when their spouse gets sick. They walk away to 'find themselves' rather than make sacrifices, go back to school, and get jobs."

Well," she reflected. "He would have done the same for me."

As much as I admired Louise and as much as I miss our "back yard fence" conversations, these chapters are about parenting, not marriage. I would not presume to guess what allowed this heroic woman to put the needs of her family above any thought for herself. That said, the subject of sacrifice does come up in my musings about parenting.

Babies cry in the middle of the night. That's what babies do. It's their job. As I am not the first to observe, some babies turn crying in the middle of the night into a career.

Change, cuddle, feed, burp. Change, cuddle, feed, burp. That pretty much covers it. If a bottle doesn't work, try burping. If burping doesn't calm the baby, go back to cuddling. Rinse and repeat.

No one would argue that a newborn needs to "suck it up," "figure it out," or "learn to soothe herself." The smart money is "err on the side of nurture." A child whose physical and emotional needs are met is more likely to grow up to be a content adult. Yet if we listen to some current parents, the needs of the kids don't even make the top ten list. The priorities are inverted: "I need to go out to the clubs every night;" "I have to work weekends so I can make payments on our second home."

I wish you every success at the club and I hope you'll invite me to your place in the mountains, but you can't have it both ways. When babies cry in the middle of the night, when toddlers need to be reassured that the world is a safe place, when children need someone to read them a story, when adolescents needs someone to sit on the couch with them and talk about nothing, when teenagers need someone to be in the house so they know they can't get away with bringing home idiot friends, parents need to be there.

If you can't make the sacrifice and sign on to do what's right for your kids, then you may need to rethink your expectations about what your kids are going to do for you. You wouldn't listen to advice from a stranger; neither will your children.

It's just that simple--as simple as Louise taking care of her dying husband for nine years.

79

Letting Go

Look, if there was any chance that you actually <u>could</u> effect positive change by micromanaging your child, then I wouldn't say a word against your way of doing things. Honest. If, by swooping in, you could help your daughter in any way, I'd give you the thumbs up and leave you alone. I'd ignore that your kid may never learn to do anything without you when you're doing everything for her. I'd overlook the psychological damage that comes from a child not being able to feel her own feelings, determine her own sense of self.

I feel the same way about different kinds of crimes. If you were at least <u>successful</u> at robbing the bank, I would try not to ask you where you got the money. The problem is, you keep getting caught. Not only do you not get to keep that sack full of hundred dollar bills from the teller's drawer, but you also keep ending up in jail. Not only are you smothering your child, but your child also isn't learning anything. Your parenting is lose/lose.

So my narrower point for today is that "lawn mower parenting" (which has replaced "helicopter parenting;" where have you been?) is ineffective at every level. By hovering on top of your kids like white on rice, nothing good happens. Consider the following note to the teacher from the mother of a fifth grader.

"I note that Samantha received a 96 because the data table for her science project was incorrect. I helped Sam construct the data table from a template on my computer and I assure you that the table was correct. Please change her grade to 100 immediately."

Ignoring for a moment the glaring question of "whose assignment is this?" let's talk about the 11-year-old. Remember the 11 year-old? Needless to say, this child is conflicted and distraught as her mother prepares to go to war. Mom will start grousing at the teacher, then go up the chain of command to bark at the school counselor, the principal, the local school board, the United States Department of Education, and ultimately the National Aeronautics and Space Administration. (Why NASA? Well, it was a *science* fair project after all.)

Mom may win the battle; the grade may end up getting changed. But mom will lost the war. If the ultimate goal is to allow her daughter to learn how to accomplish on her own, then there has been no forward progress. Will Samantha ever learn how to advocate for herself? Will she be able to determine which issues are worth pursuing with a teacher and which should be left alone? Will she be able to accept herself for who she is, a kid who constructed her own data table and got a 96?

Not likely.

Elementary school *could* be a time filled with the joy of learning. Elementary school *should* be a time filled with developmentally appropriate chances to grow and learn from missteps. Instead fifth grade is a hot mess of writhing anxiety and struggle. Mom writes nasty emails to teacher, mom screams at soccer coach; mom orchestrates every action and intrudes on every thought.

If I were a snarkier sort of author, I might be so presumptuous to suggest that mom has too much time on her hands.

Some things are worth fighting for. Some issues are beyond a child's capability to address. A 96 on a data table is not one of those things.

When stuff goes wrong at school, it's helpful for your kid to know that she has someone at home to talk to. It's helpful for her to know that someone has her back and will listen to her concerns. It's helpful for her to know that there is someone with whom she can bounce around an idea and get some support. It can only make her nervous and scared to know that the process of problem solving is going to be taken out of her hands, that someone is going to fight the wrong battle for her in the wrong way.

Listening and problem solving communicates, "I trust you and I know you can handle this." Writing notes to the teacher, swooping in and messing everything up communicates, "You are not competent to do this on your own and besides, your grades are more important that your actually learning anything."

What you communicate to your child is more important that whether she gets a 96 or 100 on her data table.

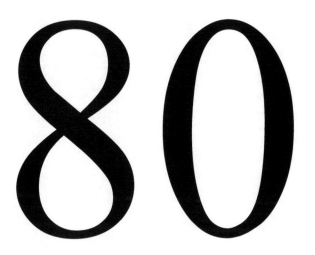

Homework: Threat or Menace? *

Even Isaac Newton, reputed to be a bright boy by any measure, believed in the transmutation of elements. Turn lead into gold? Sure, why not? Lead into gold. How hard could it be?

Turns out the process of switching from this element to that element involves the number of protons in the nucleus of the atom, concepts with which the best thinkers of the mid-17th century were

290

staggeringly unfamiliar. Newton could invent calculus and make lasting contributions to optics, whatever that is, but absent one of those billion dollar collider thingies, changing one element into another wasn't happening.

Unlike Newton who never turned lead into anything but more lead, you have the power to turn your peaceful, pleasant, functioning household into a hellish scream-fest with only one seemingly innocuous interrogatory. "Did you do your homework?" can engender a plunge into a black hole from which-speaking of physics-no light or life can ever return.

"We didn't have any homework!" "I already did my homework!" Why are you always hounding me?" are just a few of the more gentle replies from frazzled, frustrated students. At the end of which conversation-stop me if you've heard this one before-no more actual homework is done.

Remember your "friend" who is "helping" you to lose weight and be healthy by "thoughtfully" reminding you to eat right and get to the gym? Your friend many be right. We all could benefit from committing to less sugar and more cardio. But who wants to hear that shit? Especially because your "friend" with the advice is invariably a size two who runs marathons while pushing her gifted toddler in a stroller and getting promoted at her high-paying, work-from-home job. In any relationship, mentioning the same guidance more than three times in a year is nagging. Your kids feel the same way. Trust me on this one: they already know your opinion on homework.

Don't get me wrong. There may be some benefit to homework for high school kids. If homework engenders learning beyond the classroom, who am I to suggest that it seldom does? My issue is with parents *asking* about homework getting done. Is "Did you do your homework? Did you do your homework?" the revenge of the parents for the children's incessant "are we there yet" of car trips past?

Whether or not your child *learns* anything from doing homework (she doesn't-homework is about compliance, not learning) is another subject. None-the-less, it may be in your child's interest to *do* homework thus avoiding public humiliation and a GPA lower than a snake's belly in a wagon rut. If your child is going to do homework, she had better figure out how to do so on her own. Because "Do you have your day planner? Did you write down your assignments? When is your next test?" never leads to "Thanks, Mumsy. I had almost forgotten these important responsibilities. I'll get cracking in two shakes of a lamb's tail!"

Martin Cruz Smith writes about a man who breaks a hole in the ice in Siberia in February and jumps in. Whether he crawls out of the water and freezes to death in the 40 below air or stays in the water and dies of hypothermia is of little concern three minutes later because dead is dead. If parents are yelling at kids to do homework, the train is already off the track.

Typically kids who *can* do homework *do* do homework.

You see your kids as movies. I see your kids as snapshots. That is, you see your kids every day. I only connect with them every so often. But I have seen the end of the film. Here's what can happen when parents yell at high school kids to do homework:

1) Kids can come to believe that their parents' expectations are unreasonable, that their parents aren't connected to their children's abilities and limitations. And before you intone that the homework is asking him to write the definitions for and memorize 20 lousy vocabulary words not compose a violin concerto or remove his own appendix, remember that the kid has myriad other responsibilities including sports and other classes and that he may be burnt out by the end of the day.

2) The "noise" concerning homework can be so loud that other more important information is ignored or overlooked. In a "Boy Who Cried Wolf" scenario, I'd rather my kids hear "don't take drugs" than "do your homework."

3) Kids will be able to find their own meaning, make their own priorities, figure out what is important to them, individuate from their parents if the responsibility for planning, prioritizing, and doing homework remains entirely with them.

And, if I may speak frankly, you couldn't pass the final exam from the last math class you took for love or money, but your attitude about learning remains deeply embedded in your way of looking at the world. You may not remember much math, but you do remember your process of doing homework. Or as the only person ever smarter than Newton said, "Education is what remains after one has forgotten what one has learned at school."

Let the kids derive their own meaning from homework. Einstein got it right.

So can you.

* Readers of a certain age may recognize the title of this essay as having been appropriated from "National Lampoon," volume 1, number 16, 1971.

81

What are the Odds

When a slot machine pays out ten thousand dollars, sirens blare, lights flash, and young women in bathing suits crowd around to help pick up the explosion of spewing quarters. The joyful winner bathes in admiration and coins up to his ankles as joyful music plays and the crowd cheers. Gamblers at nearby machines smile and shout congratulations.

The bets that don't win, on the other hand, are not cause for celebration. Indeed, the near-silent "thunk" as the quarter slips into the bowels of the machine is the only indication that a bet has even been placed. That slot machines are now electronic rather than mechanical does not alter my argument. It's hard to know just how many "losing" quarters are noiselessly filling the entrails. A discerning observer can only note that a $250,000,000 hotel does not build itself. The money has to come from somewhere. That somewhere involves a number of inserted quarters that do NOT result is sirens, lights, and bikinis.

My subscribers are sophisticated enough to gamble only for entertainment if at all. No one reading these books believes that a slot machine is a good long-term investment or that the expected value of those fleeing quarters is more than twenty-five cents. Yet these same erudite folks have been known to gamble their children in similarly senseless ways.

Consider SAT courses. Your child's score *may* go up hundreds of points as a result of short-term intervention. Cue lights, sirens, and bikinis. Or your child's score may not improve. Thud. Thud. Thud. If your child's score does improve hundreds of points, the likelihood or her being admitted to her top choice college may improve-wattage, noise, bathing suits. Or she may not be selected at the selected select school. Again, thud. Believing that every child who takes an SAT course has a significant score improvement is akin to believing that every quarter invested in a slot machine pays ten thousand dollars. It ain't necessarily so. And believe me: the parents of the "losing" children are not talking about their score. "Yes, I invested thousands of dollars and hour after hour of my child's time, but her SAT score stayed at the same lousy 980" are words no parent ever spoke.

What about paying north of $30K/year for private day school tuition or double that amount for boarding school? If the schools are "selling" admission statistics at "top" colleges, you're being scammed. Good students are admitted to good colleges. There is no reasonable argument on this point. High schools braying about the number of their students who get good results on AP tests or get admitted to HYPS* could just as well be proclaiming "we only admit kids with high test scores to begin with." Just as a chicken is an egg's way of making another egg, students admitted to HYPS are a high school's way of justifying tuition. Not a news flash: Kids from public schools go to top colleges as well. Again, no parent ever said, "Yes, we paid a quarter million dollars for tuition at a private day school, but my child was rejected from every top college." Thud. No one brags about the quarters that don't "win."

Full disclosure One: I taught SAT courses for decades. Many of the students whom I taught had scores that improved significantly. Many did not.

Full disclosure Two: Any number of my own children attended wonderful private schools both day and boarding. At these institutions, my children learned to think critically and write well. They got moral instruction from the honor code. They learned from teachers who were exemplary in the classroom and out. They did community service, participated in athletics, and ate nutritious food. In short, their educations were extraordinary and worth every penny. But my kids didn't go to "top" colleges as a result of their good high schools any more than wiggling in your seat increases the chances of having your quarter be the one that makes the sirens blare.

Loren Pope expressed the extraordinary experience of a good college education: "The magic lies in the moral and intellectual torque that the college exerts, not the name, however hallowed it may be."

Now there's a return on investment that can't be beat.

296

82

Come and Get it!

Remember in college when four CBS blocks and two six-foot boards constituted a functional bookshelf? Two battered pots-one for simmering tomato sauce, one for making spaghetti-constituted cookware. Somebody brought salad, somebody else brought garlic bread and-voila!-let's eat. Clean up involved five minutes of scrubbing and two trips to the dumpster to empty the containers of paper plates and empty bottles.

A few years later in that first, tiny apartment, meals with friends were somewhat more sophisticated-but only somewhat. Actual furniture had replaced milk cartons, plastic plates had ousted paper, and there was an actual barbecue in the common area so grilled chicken usurped noodles. Somebody brought pasta salad and somebody else brought a dish recognizable as a dessert. Perfect! Good comestibles, good conversation, good company.

After chatting about sports, politics, relationships and how much all the guests hated their first job out of college, everybody pitched in to do the dishes. What a great evening! Who could ask for more?

Fast forward a decade or three and dinner parties with close friends are still a joy. The menu is more sophisticated and the furniture is paid for. Sure, scheduling is a little more complicated, but the basic principles of camaraderie, conversation, and closeness still prevail. Everybody talks, everybody eats, everybody helps clean up.

Imagine to the contrary that instead of being an active participant with a sense of shared purpose, you were an employee in the kitchen. "Chop those onions! Wipe that table! Hurry up there! Why isn't that salad dressing finished yet?"

Making a contribution feels good. Being told what to do, less so. Mutual endeavor working toward a common goal is part of what makes us human. Subjugation is part of what makes us monstrous.

So if you and I like pitching in and being part of something bigger than ourselves, why would we believe that our children would feel any differently?

***

298

From the time they're old enough to spill flour all over their faces and jammies to the time they make cookies for their middle school friends, kids love being part of what's happening in the kitchen. Making brownies teaches chemistry (what kind of reaction is this?) math (three eggs for one package, how many eggs for two packages?) and cooperation (whose turn is it to lick the spoon?)

Adults would rather be invited to a dinner party than be employed at one. Kids would rather be part of a process bigger than themselves than be enslaved by parents pontificating about how chores build character. Even a stray dog knows if she has been tripped over or kicked. Including kids in the process of making a family function builds stronger relationships, better families, and cleaner kitchens.

It is hardly an exaggeration to suggest that we are predisposed at a fundamental level to live in family groups. Everybody benefits when everybody pitches in. See that guy over there on the African Savannah, the one playing a violent video game by himself? He is unlikely to survive long enough to have his DNA replicated in subsequent generations. All the cool Homo habilis chicks favor the dudes who want to hang out talking about how they can't wait for proms to be invented one hundred thousand generations down the road.

Richard Dawkins suggests that our evolutionarily adaptive environment was unforgiving of the solitary guy who didn't play nice with others. Ignoring the received knowledge of previous generations had consequences in real time. "Stay away from the edge of the cliff" and "Don't eat the red berries" had meaning generations ago just like "Do you want to help make some brownies" does today.

Why was that Homo habilis over there by himself? Hard to say given how tough it is to retrieve emails from two million years ago. But maybe he was tired of being told what to do rather than participating in the common purpose of the group.

A kid today eating dinner in front of a television or alone in his room is missing out on nutrition both caloric and emotional. Allowing kids to be part of the process of making a meal and making a family is what connects them to something greater than themselves.

83

Most Famous Fictional Character

What do Benedict Cumberbatch, Robert Downey, Jr., and Basil Rathbone have in common? Tough question, don't you agree? The following information may not make the answer any more apparent: Michael Caine, Peter O'Toole, and Charlton Heston (of all people) have all done the same thing. As have Leonard Nimoy, Larry Hagman, and George C. Scott.

Stumped? Here's a hint: the fictional character most often portrayed is not, as I would have thought, Frankenstein. Nor is it Dracula. The monsters are in second and third place respectively. The winner, with more appearances in "film, television, stage, or radio" than even Frankenstein or Dracula, is Sherlock Holmes.

It is difficult to pinpoint the exact number of printed copies of the four novels and 56 short stories by Conan Doyle. A reasonable guess might be "more than Harry Potter, fewer than the Bible." In short, millions of copies.

Why the enduring popularity? The malevolent villains, the wealthy supplicants, the wry banter between Holmes and Watson all have their appeal. But the "aha moment" is especially seductive for me. All my neurons light up when Holmes explains how he solved the crime. "Yes, of course!" gives me pleasure. And then I go on: "I could have figured that out-if only I had devoted hours of uninterrupted study to learning all the different strains of tobacco sold around London." "Of course," I exclaim. "The mud on the murderer's boots *obviously* came from Ipswitch! Anyone who dedicated endless time and attention to studying mud under a microscope would know that."

You and I might not be lucky enough to have been bitten by a radioactive spider or born on Krypton but IF we committed our lives to studying tobacco, mud and the "agony" column of the London Times, we could solve singular crimes that would leave the heads of European countries expressing speechless thanks. Holmes was a man like you or I only more insightful and with more time on his hands. Holmes was successful not only because of superior intellect but also because of intense study. He made inferences based on knowledge painstakingly acquired.

302

Fast-forward a century and a bit to a popular TV series. Like Holmes, the protagonist of "Limitless" is able to make connections, bring together disparate information, and solve complex crimes.

By taking a pill.

No study required. He remembers everything he's ever seen, heard, or smelled based on digesting a clear pill.

Mind you, this essay is not my frequent screed about the disadvantages or tinkering with the brain chemistry of your minor child. Long-term readers are familiar with how convinced this author is that psycho-stimulants and SSRIs are over-prescribed for young ones. My readers know my opinion on recreational abuse of prescription medications. My interest today focuses on heroes who don't do the work, but get the grades anyway. Brian Finch doesn't study mud, tobacco, or society pages. He just brings the information together chemically.

On "Shameless," "Lip" cuts class, throws a chair through a window, and gets expelled from school but passes the AP exam because he "read the book a couple years ago." Viewers see him drink beer; they don't see him study.

In the real world where so many of our children actually reside, endless hours of study are required to achieve proficiency. Smart kids put in just as many hours to achieve mastery because they take harder courses.

Modeling sober attention to learning will benefit all children. Exposing them to television shows where characters with modest ability and less motivation solve crimes and excel on tests will not.

At what age should we read with our kids rather than allow them to devote their lives to screens? As Benedict Cumberbatch, Basil Rathbone, or Robert Downey, Jr. would agree: "Elementary!"

84

This is Your Life

Look, any relationship requires give and take, don't you thing? A parent has a relationship with a child, a married person has a relationship with a spouse, and a reader has a relationship with an author.

You and I have been connected by these newsletters for getting on six years now. As it happens, this is the 300th blog post and the last

304

chapter in the third book. So I'm asking your indulgence as my ADD brain bounces around like a Ping-Pong ball in a snowstorm. It may be tough to trace the path of the Ping-Pong ball in real time, but come the Spring it will be easy to find. Admittedly, the analogy breaks down in that nobody needs a stupid Ping-Pong ball given how much work there is to do after the snow melts and why would you bother looking for the darn thing anyway when you could just go buy a package of Ping-Pong balls for a few bucks, but you get what I mean. Anyway, here is a sentence taken from an SAT administered in 1980. (Yes, I have a copy of every SAT administered for the past 35 years. No, I don't want to talk about it.)

"... The question is not whether *The Clouds* should be read in Greek or in English: the question is whether it should be read in English or not read at all."

Or deciphered from ETS-ese: it's better for kids to read classics in translation than not read classics at all.

The other side of the coin is "Well, if the kids know they can just read the translations, why would they learn classical languages?" I am going to call this argument the "tough nuggies" approach to teaching and parenting. Yes, in a perfect world, all children would learn Latin and Greek. Should you find said perfect world, give me a call and I'll meet you.

I have been accused of being too willing to lower my expectations. My running career may serve as a useful example. Ideally, I would like to run a mile in just under nine minutes then run another mile in just under nine minutes and so on until I had run 26 miles at just under nine minutes each. My total time of three hours and 55 minutes would allow me, at age 60, to qualify to run the Boston Marathon, a goal I have been attending to, on and off, for the past 36 years. Like Edison said before he actually did invent the light bulb, "I have not failed. I have just found 10,000 ways that won't work." Similarly, I know 18 ways NOT to run a Boston qualifying time.

In "tough nuggy" world, I wouldn't keep running these disappointing marathons. Realizing that I am never going to frigging qualify, I would put down *The Clouds* or hang up my running shoes. Not being able to run properly, I would not run at all.

Which brings me--"finally" you might say--to my point about parenting for this week: I wish my kids would do the dishes, mow the lawn, clean their rooms. What's more, I wish they would do these chores without my help. In a perfect world--there's that phrase again--the kids would wake up early and make me breakfast.

I am not holding my breath.

Instead, I get up and the kids and I make breakfast together. Frequently, we bump into one another in our absurdly small kitchen as we hurry to find the eggs. How hard could it be to find the eggs? It's a refrigerator for goodness sake, not a haystack. The eggs have got to be in there somewhere. Occasionally, harsh words are spoken as the children and I frenetically scramble to find backpacks, shoes, and car keys so there is some chance that we can get to school before the end of the Pleistocene and avoid the "death stare" from the woman who gives us the "late to class" note. Again.

Remember that guy in "Chariots of Fire" who had his servant pour champagne into those glasses placed on the hurdles? Then, with the castle and the thousand acre estate in the background, Lord Lindsey leaps perfectly over each barrier so effortlessly that not a drop is spilled? I'm betting Lord Lindsey's kids got to school on time. You gotta figure Lord Lindsey's kids learned Latin and Greek and didn't get away with reading the translations either.

I wish Lord Lindsey every success. But I'm going to live the life I've got not the life of a guy on an estate with champagne on the hurdles. I'm going to keep running even though I'm never going to run fast enough to qualify for Boston; I'm going to keep jostling and joking

306

with my kids as we try to find the eggs. (There. By your hand. If it was a snake, you'd be dead.)

This is the life I have with my kids. It might not be the life I envisioned, there might not be much champagne and less Greek in this life, but it'll do.

Made in the USA
San Bernardino, CA
31 August 2016